San Jose Christian College Library
790 S. 12th St., P. O. Box 1090
San Jose, California 95108

William Jessup University
Library
333 Sunset Blvd.
Rocklin, Ca 95765

The Responsible Pulpit

San Jose Christian College Library
790 S. 12th St., P. O. Box 1090
San Jose, California 95108

The Responsible Pulpit

James Earl Massey

San Jose Christian College Library
790 S. 12th St., P. O. Box 1090
San Jose, California 95108

 WARNER PRESS
Anderson, Ind.

THE RESPONSIBLE PULPIT

Copyright © 1974 by James Earl Massey

Published by Warner Press, Inc.

Anderson, Ind. 46011

With but few exceptions the Scripture quotations used in the text of this book are from the Revised Standard Version of the Bible, copyrighted 1946 and 1952 by the Division of Christian Education, NCCUSA.

Library of Congress Cataloging in Publication Data

Massey, James Earl

   The responsible pulpit.

   Includes bibliographical references.

   1. Reading. 2. Clergy—Religious life.
I. Title.
BV4211.2.M28   251   74-939
ISBN 0-87162-169-X

Printed in the United States of America.

In memory of
JOHN B. RICHARDS
my first pastor
and
in appreciation to
DR. RAYMOND SAMUEL JACKSON
under whose pastoral ministry
I received my call to preach.

Contents

I. A RESPONSIBLE FAITH
  Concerning Jesus Christ 15

II. A RESPONSIBLE SELF
  Confronting Life 31

III. THE SERMON
  Responsible Hermeneutics 53

IV. THE SERMON
  Responsible Homiletics 67

V. CONTENT
  Insights from the Preaching of Jesus . . . 93

VI. DELIVERY
  Insights from the Black Preaching Tradition . . 101

  EPILOGUE
  "Striving for the Mastery" 113

Preface

It has been an honor, highly prized, to fulfill engagements as preacher or lecturer to seminary audiences, ministerial assemblies, and to guide working pastors in sermon clinics and workshops on preaching. This brief book has resulted from such occasions. It has been a work of love to share some of my experiences, insights, and convictions with so many others intent to fulfill their ministry as preachers. Critical questions, searching comments, and encouraging responses during those occasions of service have helped to determine the lines along which this book has been written. The title and theme are not merely academic, and the stress upon the need for responsible pulpits in our churches is not without evident reason.

One of the most pressing needs at present in the churches across the land is an understanding and acceptance of responsibility, and this is true "from the pulpit to the door," to repeat an oft-used phrase from the Black Church tradition. Responsibility is always *to* someone and it is always *for* something, and there is a dynamic connection between these two aspects of demand. A renewal of the preacher's sense of responsibility to Christ can lead to a renewal of the church which is his body. This book reflects some of my own thought, study, and speaking on this matter. No attempt is made here to deal with preaching along all of the formal lines of concern, but rather to review the imperative for preaching with a responsible faith, a committed selfhood, a hermeneutical honesty

THE RESPONSIBLE PULPIT

that honors the Word of God, and homiletical competence that honors those who hear us address them.

Many persons have helped me to review and refine my thought on the theme treated in this book, as my notes will readily indicate. Besides these, I am especially grateful to Dr. Randolph Crump Miller, Horace Bushnell Professor of Christian Nurture, Yale University Divinity School, who read Chapter III and offered wise counsel toward improving it; Dr. Evans Edgar Crawford, Dean of Rankin Chapel and Professor of Social Ethics at Howard University School of Religion, who offered timely encouragement and stimulating discussion when I made known to him my intent to enrich this book through insights from the life and preaching tradition of the Black Church. These two mentors have been kind critics, and I thank them for their helpful suggestions; whatever fault remains locked within these pages must be charged only to me.

In gratitude for the invitations to formally treat the work of preaching, I offer here a word of thanks to the leaders of the institutions where I have dealt with this theme and related aspects: Huntington College, Huntington, Indiana; North Park Theological Seminary, Chicago, Illinois; Virginia Union University School of Religion, Richmond, Virginia; Winebrenner Theological Seminary, Findlay, Ohio; Associated Mennonite Biblical Seminaries, Elkhart, Indiana; Christian Theological Seminary, Indianapolis, Indiana; Malone College, Canton, Ohio.

Nor do I forget the congregations which have both demanded much from me and given so much in return. For more than twenty years I have deeply lived and learned while serving the pulpit and parish demands of Metropolitan Church in Detroit, Michigan. My work as campus minister at Anderson College across the past four years, especially preaching in All-Campus Chapel Services, has also kept me sensitive and responsible to God and man.

The final casting of these pages was done during a period of leisure made possible through a Danforth Foundation grant upon my appointment as an Underwood Fellow 1972-73. I heartily

Preface

express my appreciation to the Danforth Foundation officials for their interest and confidence in my campus ministry. Finally, appreciation is also due Mrs. Eileen Clay, my secretary, who skillfully typed the manuscript—"deciphering" my written code—and made the completion of this work less tedious.

JAMES EARL MASSEY

Anderson College School of Theology
Anderson, Indiana
January, 1973

Chapter I

A RESPONSIBLE FAITH
Concerning Jesus Christ

IT WAS THE FIRST day of the week. It was that day when the report first circulated that the body of Jesus was missing from its tomb. Two disciples of Jesus were talking in sadness as they walked toward Emmaus from Jerusalem. Their high hopes for Jesus had not been fulfilled: he had been put to death, crucified. These two men, like the other disciples of Jesus, had lived a weekend in felt disappointment. But the record about their journey tells us that "While they were talking and discussing together, Jesus himself drew near and went with them" (Luke 24:15), unrecognized at first, and certainly unanticipated. Jesus joined their conversation—with a leading question: "What is this conversation which you are holding with each other as you walk?" (v. 17a). The two friends paused to recapitulate the sad talk done between them, and the total experience soon deepened as the three conversed.

Cleopas, one of the two friends, was a ready conversant. He supplied answers to queries the Stranger now with them put forth. The answers he gave betrayed his deepest feelings and his frustrated hope. It was a sad and disillusioned Cleopas who explained, "But we had hoped that he was the one to redeem Israel" (v. 21a). The hope was certainly political, based upon strong desire that Israel know self-rule again.

THE RESPONSIBLE PULPIT

The atmosphere must have become charged increasingly with feeling as the other disciple added his word. He joined Cleopas in telling the Stranger about what had happened to Jesus. Then together they dared to mention the report, confirmed by some of the men of their group, that the body of Jesus was missing from its tomb since early morning. The increased feeling is understandable. The two friends must have waited in uneasiness for some reaction from the listening Stranger. How would he react to such talk? How would he regard such a report? What would he think of *them*—or those friends who had astounded them with the report that Jesus was alive again?

The Stranger did speak finally, and he spoke with finality. By the time the three reached Emmaus he had broadened the two friends' understanding of the Old Testament. He had explained the suffering and death of the Christ. The wording at Luke 24:27, *diermeneusen autois,* "He explained to them," suggests that the speaking Stranger offered his two hearers a quite pointed commentary on various Old Testament passages. He served them as hermeneut and by exegetical comments clarified prophetic passages about the sufferings of Christ. It was an emphatic action on his part, and what he said to them formed the foundation—teaching by which Jesus became the center of the message of faith. The two disciples sensed the numinous quality of the experience they were having in his company. When they reached Emmaus and sat to share an evening meal, the Stranger's words and actions were finally recognized as those of Jesus himself. The two "recognized him; and he vanished out of their sight" (24:31). The recognition was an objective historical fact in their experience. That recognition and experience had indelible effects upon the character and concern of these men. Together with the other disciples, these eyewitnesses of the risen Jesus soon found themselves at new frontiers in their knowledge and understanding of the work of God in his life and in their lives. They embraced a new understanding of Jesus of Nazareth. Their subsequent preaching about Jesus proclaimed him as the Christ.

A Responsible Faith

These first witnesses did not fully understand all that was happening to them. There was mystery about it, to be sure, but there was no doubt about what they were experiencing *in connection with Jesus* in their lives. After the resurrection they had a new understanding of the Cross-event. What these witnesses said and did showed that the character and claims of Jesus had actively engaged their lives, that he was still shaping their history and was guiding them in shaping a new history in their time on God's order. Forever afterward those witnesses knew that the basic test of their living would be how they treated his confidence in them—that is to say, they sensed the responsibility that their experiences with Jesus laid upon them.

Jesus Is Still at the Center

The most basic test of the Christian minister still is what he believes, says, and does concerning Jesus. What teachings about Jesus can he proclaim with full faith and responsible thought? What is his personal depth of faith about what Jesus himself taught? How does his life relate to the message he speaks about Jesus? How persistent and focused is his intent to speak *of* Christ and *for* him? Several articles in popular magazines across the last decade or more presumed to inform us about the beliefs of the then-coming generation of parish ministers. Some of the "disclosures" were somewhat sententious and misleading; some other articles rightly criticized views that are not representative of the Christian faith. It is not necessary here to discuss the many details in the articles, but it has been interesting to see the reader replies to those articles. Those replies have shown that public interest in what ministers believe remains strong. And rightly so.

The preacher is rightfully expected to exercise his mind and delve into the New Testament witness about Jesus. He is then expected to develop certain convictions from his encounter with the records. He is expected to wrestle with texts that bristle with difficulties and seek logical solutions for problem passages. Responsible preaching can never result unless he faces the total New Testament witness and thinks with seriousness about that witness. The Christian preacher is rightfully expected to be a responsible man, using faith to seek more understanding and not structure in doubt a system by which to talk around or ignore certain paradoxical elements in the records about Jesus. The witness is given: it issued from reporters backed by experience and faith. That witness from them is best handled by men who, in ready faith, are willing to stretch their minds and lives to honestly receive it. Called to preach Christ, we shall forever be tested by the biblical report itself, the need to believe what we are handling, and the utter greatness of the One with whom we have to do.

Christology is still the signal testing ground of the preacher's faith, intentions, and sense of responsibility. His preaching will show where he stands. It will show whether he is a spokesman of the given Word or whether he is substituting his own formulations in place of the Faith. Christian preaching must always be measured by the place Jesus Christ holds in it.

The Saving Person

The apostolic leaders preached Christ. Perhaps the best commentary on their preaching is an unabridged concordance that illustrates the extent to which his name and concerns were on their lips. Those leaders were always making claims for Christ. They were forever addressing men in his name. They knew that Jesus was decisive for man's need of salvation. They trusted his confessed mission—and believed in him as the unique Son sent by God to handle that mission.

In our day the mission of Jesus is being discussed in comparative terms with the emphases and claims of the great religions of the world. Such study is fitting, important, and imperative. Jesus himself is also under discussion: great interest attaches to his attitude toward life, his faith toward God, his self-understanding, his claims, and his eschatological views, among other things. These,

A Responsible Faith

too, are logical concerns for study. Still other studies have yielded an increased knowledge about the first century period, the environment of Judaism and Rome, the nationalistic concerns of the nation Israel with its groups and movements. These studies are likewise invaluable. Heritage and history, environment and group expectations must all come under strict view in any attempt to trace clearly his steps and better understand his stride. But true insight into Jesus and his mission demands a confrontation with the apostolic message about him. That is the admitted purpose of the Gospels. That is the open thrust of the preaching recounted in the Acts. That is the basis for the teaching in the Epistles.

As for the Gospels, they were produced for kerygmatic and polemical reasons. The evangelists did not write as reporters on a dead issue but as witnesses about the living revelation of God in Jesus. A crucial history was in their minds, and in their hearts. *Jesus* had come, lived, died, and he had risen again. Those writers listed and linked the details about that history, sometimes topically, sometimes in chronological order, but those details were a remembered and regarded part of an experienced drama of divine life. The Gospel writers witnessed to a special history within general history. They reported an ordained history by which general history gains meaning. They wrote to present some unique claims about Jesus as Christ. Some modern historiographers have complained that in the Gospels materials and interpretation are too conjoined to permit a clear picture of history. They have lamented that events there are all overshadowed by idea and interpretation. They have called attention to a "faultiness" in the accounts due to zeal for reporting, compounded by the haze of distance after the events. They have sought to isolate the techniques employed to serve the truth. They have sought to separate what is legend from what is the real stuff of his life. The question is still being asked: Is a *clear* picture of the events really possible at this point in history? Meanwhile the materials continue to confront us— with strong words, adequate for faith, about that saving Person. We turn now to reflect on the witness of these strong words.

THE RESPONSIBLE PULPIT

The Apostolic Message

1. The first Christian preachers preached about Jesus Christ as the unique *Son of God*. The Gospel stories of his birth clearly teach something more than that Jesus was a godly son of one Joseph and Mary. The Gospel picture and New Testament teachings are much wider than that. The Fourth Gospel speaks of Jesus as the "only Son" (*monogenes huios,* 1:18), stressing his uniqueness as to kind. That same Gospel reports Jesus speaking of himself in the same way (cf. John 3:16, 18).

It is true that "Son" appears earlier in Hebrew history in connection with the nation under God, ". . . you have seen how the Lord your God bore you, as a man bears his son, in all the way that you went until you came to this place" (Deut. 1:31), but the New Testament witness about Jesus involves far more than a representative relation with God. The New Testament picture is much wider. Again the Fourth Gospel, "he had come from God and was going to God" (13:3), with whom he had shared a glory before the world began (cf. 17:5). Here was a relationship at once personal, transcendental, and eternal. There was something more in the life of Jesus than a high capacity to bear transcendental elements in his character. There was something more in Jesus than a spirit of radical obedience; something more than exemplary conduct showing a strong relation to that about which he spoke; something more than a concern for an *imitatio Dei*. The first Christian preachers experienced Jesus as one "full of grace and truth" and "glory, glory as of the only Son from the Father" (John 1:14). They preached about him as the Word become flesh.

2. The first Christian preachers concerned themselves with the theme of "Christ crucified." They were the first to admit that the picture of Christ on a cross seems to suggest a problem and not solve one. The picture *is* problematic, as Paul admitted: "For Jews demand signs and Greeks seek wisdom, but we preach Christ crucified, a stumbling-block to Jews and folly to Gentiles" (1 Cor. 1:22-23). The Jews saw the cross as abhorrent. The Greeks

A Responsible Faith

viewed Paul's explanation of the cross as absurd: Why, then, did Paul so preach? He tells us: "Christ [is] the power of God and the wisdom of God" (1:24); that is, Christian preaching is not calculated to satisfy or please human notions but to meet human need; it is not a mere argument but an agency for salvation.

The "word of the cross" (1:18) is a saving word. That is its service. It confronts the hearer with the fundamental revealing event in gospel history, namely that "Christ died for us" (Rom. 5:8). Despite its "original offense," the "word of the cross" vividly points to the sacrificial death of Christ on our behalf. The fact calls us to account; it strives with us, reproving, judging, yet offering hope. The cross is the sign of God's love—and man's sin. It is judgment, but it is also our justification. It is the decisive word that calls us to decision. The word of the cross is a revealing, redemptive, and ruling word. It reveals because it is part of a larger, longer story and divine plan. It is redemptive because it assigns our sins to *his* volunteered and vicarious sacrifice. It is ruling because of the constraint its meaning makes upon our spirits.

The New Testament writings are especially Cross-conscious. In a very definite sense the "word of the cross" summarizes the apostolic witness about the importance of Jesus to the world. Involving as it does atonement, expiation, justification, and propitiation, the word of the cross is the crucial doctrine in the Christian faith. There is no true understanding of the mission of Jesus without a right understanding of the cross. The theme of Jesus entering into the Cross-event, with saving purpose, is the great theme in the New Testament.

John H. Jowett once remarked that "You cannot drop the big themes and create great saints."[1] The first Christian preachers did not give scant place to the big theme of Calvary. The sacrifice of Jesus is a big theme. It is a doctrine of depth. It is not easily handled, being so manysided. To be sure, the first Christian preachers did proclaim the resurrection—by which the cross was seen in a wider context of victory and vindication, but their preaching always started with the word of the cross, and they spoke with conviction using urgent and meaningful metaphors to put the theme with clarity and convincement. The word of the cross judged all their topics and provided background for all other words. That word is also a measure by which to test our preaching.

Joseph Parker wrote about how he felt under the test of the word of the cross. He stood convinced that that word "is the one supreme subject of an inspired Christian ministry."[2] The preaching of the cross is not just one theme among many others. It is *the* leading theme by which all the rest of our preaching is informed, corrected, chastened, purified, and empowered. It is the specific standard under which Christian preaching goes forward in the world. It is the standard by which our New Testament materials came to us. The whole New Testament is an extensive interpretation on what the cross means. The imagery that discusses the cross varies from book to book, ranging from simple metaphors to typological treatments of Leviticus 16 (as in Hebrews and 1 Peter). But while the imagery and illustrative materials differ, the repetition of the stable theme is unmistakable.

The achievement of Jesus through his cross is in constant view in the New Testament. What is true about the New Testament must be so also about our sermons: the meaning of the cross must be a constant. Paul's declaration is at once primary. We must preach Christ crucified. I need hardly add that the word *crucified* (*estauromenon,* 1 Cor. 1:23) is the perfect participle, suggesting that our message is not just about Christ as one who has been crucified but one whose present life and ministry are influenced by that all-important event. The determinative importance of this truth allows no shallow view of sin in our preaching. That determinative word of the cross does not lack in power to inspire hope for salvation from sin and the wrath of God against sin. Paul rightly explained that "Since, therefore, we are now justified by his blood, much more shall we be saved by him from the wrath of God" (Rom. 5:9).

3. The first Christian preachers proclaimed the *risen Christ.* Interestingly enough, the bulk of the Jews who first heard them

A Responsible Faith

preach this message of resurrection did not reject it as absurd or impossible. The doctrine of resurrection was not essentially novel nor incredible to them. Although at the time these men were preaching no final settlement had been made in Judaic thought about personal resurrection, there was such an abundance of teaching concerning the hope of resurrection that the Christian doctrine was quite plausible to many Jewish hearers. Gentile hearers were skeptical at first hearing: as those at Athens who, of philosophical bent, "mocked" (*echleuazon,* Acts 17:32), while others wished to hear more about the new teaching *because* it was new; still others, however, believed the message and they moved from questions of logic—the fact of physical decay, etc.—to a learning for new life in God. The Acts and the epistolary literature give sufficient indication that the resurrection, as possibility and expectation, was never seriously questioned by the Jewish members in the early church but only by the Gentiles. The lengthy discussion in 1 Corinthians 15 shows Paul's attempt to answer some questions raised in Corinth about the resurrection: and Paul's treatment of the doctrine sought to press home to his critics the utter inadequacy of any unbiblical framework into which one would be tempted to comprise this doctrine.

The first Christian preachers knew the resurrection of Jesus as historical fact. They stood humble beneath the evident mystery of the fact while they boldly proclaimed its meaning, and lived by its power. As Christian preachers we, too, must affirm the resurrection, knowing that it is an event that is fixed in history, holding promise and potency of eternal dimensions.

4. The New Testament records show that the first Christian preachers proclaimed Christ as *the exalted and determinative Person in all creation and history.* The New Testament word is brief but full: "Jesus Christ is Lord" (Phil. 2:11). The declaration is writ large on the pages of every book. The risen Jesus bears unquestionable authority: "All authority in heaven and on earth has been given to me" (Matt. 28:18). The Christian community knew this: thus such devotion to him, such doctrines regarding him,

THE RESPONSIBLE PULPIT

and such development under his living guidance. The early preachers did not lack direction, nor did the church. He was with them as "the way, and the truth, and the life" (John 14:6a). As for the development of the church under his living guidance, he called, prepared, and sent leaders to its need. As Paul explained it: "And his gifts were that some should be apostles, some prophets, some evangelists, some pastors and teachers, for the equipment of the saints, for the work of ministry, for building up the body of Christ" (Eph. 4:11-12). The destiny of the church is through his care: "I will build my church, and the powers of death shall not prevail against it" (Matt. 16:18b). Here is a further word, about a further time and experience: "Father, I desire that they also, whom thou hast given me, may be with me where I am, to behold my glory which thou hast given me in thy love for me before the foundation of the world" (John 17:24). Jesus is our Lord!

But that lordship is wider than the church; it embraces all creation and history. Paul dwells on this point again and again. The Revelation also makes the point plain when it shows Jesus as the Lamb before the throne handling the scroll of controlled history. That Lamb has plain death marks beneath its throat, "having been slain" (*esphagmenon,* 5:6), but it stands before the throne alive, alert, and with authoritative bearing, to deal with the world for God. He holds the scroll of divine will. He alone can enact its prescriptions. He stands between God and men—to bring them together. "For there is one God, and there is one mediator between God and men, the man Christ Jesus, who gave himself as a ransom for all, the testimony to which was borne at the proper time" (1 Tim. 2:5-6). "For this," Paul went on to say, "I was appointed a preacher and apostle . . ." (v. 7a). Jesus is the determinative person in history and for eternity. "And there is salvation in no one else, for there is no other name under heaven given among men by which we must be saved" (Acts 4:12).

5. The first Christian preachers made the emphatic claim that *Jesus Christ is both present and coming.* They believed and experienced his word, "I am with you always, to the close of the age"

A Responsible Faith

(Matt. 28:20b), while they trusted his promise "I will come again and will take you to myself, that where I am you may be also" **(John 14:3).**

Present—but coming: this expression holds within itself two vital truths for Christian experience and hope. The New Testament speaks much about Christ being present and available through his Spirit. This truth is of perennial significance for both the individual Christian and the total church. This mystical stress explains the glow and warmth of our experience; it also grants to worship a depth of affection, moral persuasion, spiritual relation, and contagion. It is not mere formality that everything during Christian worship takes place in the name of Jesus Christ: prayer is offered in his name; preaching is done in his stead and to his honor; singing—that action of "making melody to the Lord with all your heart" (Eph. 5:19), sacraments, indeed every word and deed gain depth "in the name of our Lord Jesus," as we are "giving thanks to God the Father through him" (Col. 3:17). The Lord's Supper permits us a backward look upon his work for us and a forward view to his coming for us, blending in one great symbolism his present availability and his future coming. Both emphases meet us again and again in the New Testament.

Paul was especially sensitive to this blend of emphases. There are passages where he speaks quite longingly about being "with Christ," and passages where he speaks of the present glories of being "in Christ." It appears that his sense of being "in Christ" was so strong that sometimes even the present seemed much like the future to come. His original and unique phrase "in Christ" has been subjected to the most technical scrutiny and imaginative interpretation. The phrase is admittedly mystical, yet Paul always used it practically. The phrase grew out of Paul's experience of the presence of Christ. It became his expression for the realization by which he daily lived. Paul knew that Christ was with him: for this presence was a stubborn and supporting fact during perils, controversies, burdensome tasks, and troubling tests. Paul's phrase "in Christ" is a symbol he contributed to the theology then taking

THE RESPONSIBLE PULPIT

shape in the growing church. It was a central conviction of his own Christian experience. It was the frame of reference for his life. The phrase does not suggest any absorption into Christ, but rather a vital alliance and agreement with him. Thus Paul's strong words: "I can do all things in him who strengthens me" (Phil. 4:13).

For both Paul and us the available presence of Christ guarantees comfort and confidence. It also means that we are constantly confronted by him. It means that we are never alone. Christ *is* present with us. Present indeed, either approving or alertly judging by his life. This confrontation is important for us. It helps us to keep the picture of Christ without distortion and our experience with him from diminishing.

Frederic W. Farrar returned from a trip to Palestine enthused to write a life of Christ. "I returned more than ever confirmed in the wish to tell the full story of the Gospels in such a manner and with such illustrations as . . . might serve to enable at least the simple and the unlearned to understand and enter into the human surroundings of the life of the Son of God."[3] His enthusiasm had its way; he wrote the story. Others have visited Palestine and written about it, impressed with the adventure of following the footsteps of the Master in even a physical way. But all have known that there is a vast difference between a Palestinean road and the real Way of the Nazarene. The real journey is far more demanding, and more adventurous still. It demands his presence with us. It demands that we be "in Christ." Preaching takes on power when we are there.

But there is also the other emphasis, the expected *parousia* of Christ. The New Testament imagery about this appearance is quite colorful. It is also complex. But we do get the message: Christ is to appear. Modern man understandably raises questions about the *how* of the event, nurtured as he is in a strongly scientific and epistemological question-setting. The descriptive language about this climatic event is indeed complex, an acknowledged blend of literal and figurative elements. But the promise, the truth, and the impact of the fact are quite vivid for handling and belief. The

A Responsible Faith

vocabulary that deals with this is necessarily one of vision for it points to an occurrence. A uniquely new *kairos* is in view.

Truth Beyond Measure

Some preachers find themselves severely restricted in their preaching themes and emphases because they seek to handle only what they can see as logically proportioned. It is true that life teaches us to measure things, to test those things by some standard, interpret them, and arrange them in our thought and living after due examination. This measuring and testing and interpretation involves the use of some principle of proportion and rule of relationship. We must of necessity consider relations, dimensions, reason, and boundaries. But seeing things in proportion demands another factor: the ability to truly perceive. Both our understanding and our faith are quite dependent upon *how* we view.

As for the elements of the faith we proclaim—that "faith which was once for all delivered [*hapax paradotheise*] to the saints" (Jude 3): some of those elements will by their very character continue to defy all attempts to encase them in exact theories. It will always remain difficult to know fully the structure of *his* life and the full dimensions of *his* history. The very reports make it difficult for us to proceed so critically since we do not hold in our hands a story of static form and closed relations.

The New Testament makes emphatic claims for Jesus Christ. Some of those claims do not fit into a "logically proportioned" scheme *except in connection with him as the Christ*. The reports about his birth can hardly be "explained and clarified" except in this manner. The same must be said about the resurrection reports. Supernaturalism confronts us in both instances. Supernaturalism is a distinct element in the New Testament accounts. Attempts to tidy up the New Testament by removing such particularities are by necessity ill-fated: the particularities are related to *him*.

One must agree that there are points at which the New Testament terminology must be submitted to our modern neighbors in

THE RESPONSIBLE PULPIT

contemporary thought forms; some of the concepts familiar to men of that ancient time *are* quite obscure to our modern thought. But it is one thing to adapt our terms while it is an altogether different and serious matter to change the substance of the message itself. The preacher is under judgment to find terms that will adequately expose the given message and not obscure it. The emphatic claims about Jesus Christ must not be diluted but declared. The declaration must by all means be clearly put, competently handled, and compassionately spoken; but even if our idioms are not always biblical, our message *must* be. In our need to be contemporary we must not cease to be Christian. In the quest for competence we must watch against improper assumption and crippling presuppositions. Our message is ordained. The elements of paradox found in it are a part of *its* logic. The unsettling elements of particularity are a part of its substance. Mascall's words are forcefully plain and relevant: "there is no valid ground for the failure of nerve which has stampeded many contemporary theologians into a total intellectual capitulation to their secular environment."[4] The grandeur of the gospel *is* the particularity of Jesus Christ and his meaning under God. It is still as Paul explained, that "faith comes from what is heard, and what is heard comes by the preaching of Christ" (Rom. 10:17).

The truly Christian preacher will speak out of his own faith to elicit faith: lacking this, a man falls under the judgmental word of Jesus against the unbelieving (but "learned") Sadducees, "You are wrong [*planasthe,* off-course, roaming, seduced], because you know neither the scriptures nor the power of God" (Matt. 22:29).

The preacher must of all men answer that question of questions about Jesus: "What do you think of the Christ? Whose son is he?" (Matt. 22:42). The preacher's life depends upon his answer, and his answer depends upon his faith. That one question will forever test our deepest convictions, the slant of our training, the spirit of our service, and our fundamental loyalties. Our answer to that question will reveal us either as misguided professionals or as true servants of God "for Jesus' sake."

A Responsible Faith

A Message of Consequence

The New Testament message concerning Jesus Christ is a message of consequence, growing out of a history of consequence. The story about him is based upon the action initiated by God in and through him. That history is both causal and creative, with effects that deal with life here and now *and* in the life to come. The history of Jesus is, therefore, crisis history, for his life will mean for us either judgment or joy. His history is conclusive: It will not be repeated, yet it does not end. Jesus came at a datable time, involved himself in the disciplines of history, but for eternal reasons. The claims he made and the functions he carried out go well beyond the history we know. Edgar P. Dickie has written, "A faith which rests *only* on history will not stand against the *facts* of history. The only thing that can overcome the world is that which cannot be explained in terms of the world."[5] "In Jesus we have a fact that shatters logic."[6] In Jesus we have the Christ of God, the unique one who gives us revelation, faith, demand, redemption, promised fulfillment, and hope.

NOTES

1. Arthur Porritt, *John Henry Jowett* (New York: George H. Doran Co., 1925), p. 127.
2. *Studies in Texts* (New York: Funk and Wagnalls Co., n.d.) Vol. II, p. vii.
3. *The Life of Christ* (Boston: Estes and Lauriat), p. 6.
4. See E. L. Mascall, *The Secularisation of Christianity:* An Analysis and a Critique (London: Darton, Longman and Todd, 1965), p. 282.
5. *Revelation and Response* (New York: Charles Scribner's Sons, 1938), p. 139.
6. *Ibid.,* p. 247.

Chapter II

A RESPONSIBLE SELF
Confronting Life

PAUL S. REES, in a winsome, devotional, and scholarly volume on Philippians, has given us some worthy insights about both that writing and Paul, its author. At his exposition of Philippians 2:5, Rees pauses in especial reflection, confessing: "Here we enter the depths. This passage is oceanic, where the fathoms are countless and the tides are measureless."[1] That Hymn to Christ in Philippians is indeed a depth passage. He who studies recent literature on the passage is heir to some interesting views and leads which help him to *classify* it: as a Pauline Christology,[2] or as an early hymn Paul borrowed from the primitive church,[3] or as a descent/ascent myth of the Divine Hero in Gnostic thought,[4] or as a reflection of the gospel story emphasizing the redemptive victory wrought by Christ.[5] But beyond any proper classification of the passage stands the practical and theological point it makes. Something distinct and important is in view as Paul says of Jesus that "he emptied himself" (*heauton ekenosen,* 2:7).[6] Philippians 2:5-11 does make us "enter the depths," because however we classify that passage it mainly highlights the responsible behavior of Jesus to God. The passage was written to make a firm moral appeal with considerations which bear directly upon our lives as Christians: *Jesus knew how to confront and handle life in the flesh.* He ac-

THE RESPONSIBLE PULPIT

cepted his God-given creatureliness. He accepted the demands and dependences of creatureliness and handled them with discipline to the honor of God. He confronted life in the flesh and, as Wayne E. Oates has put it, "decisively accepted his own humanity."[7] This whole theme is crucial for understanding Christ and ourselves, ourselves as men under divine trust to invest ourselves (unlike Adam) in self-abnegating conduct and accept (like Jesus) the divine lines for our life.

The Hymn to Christ is a lesson on what follows when we face up to human life on God's terms, accept life under God in the world, and live by faith decisions. The passage speaks majestically about Jesus' characteristic attitude of open obedience, and that is exactly why it speaks so crucially to us.

Jesus accepted his God-given creatureliness. The strength of this act of acceptance comes out in the fact that he fully turned to God in trust as a son. Jesus thus escaped a debilitating egoism and lived by that healthy dependence we rightly classify as true faith. All of this is certainly mirrored in Paul's statement that Jesus was "obedient" (*hupekoos,* Phil. 2:8) to God. Even when he contemplated the threat and fact of death on a cross, Jesus refused to assert his humanity against the will of God. He dared to will what God willed, and that for him meant facing the depths, the very lowest depths. Jesus remained in a man's place, but as an obedient man, fully open to life and fully subject to God. His obedience speaks searchingly to us. In accepting his humanity, Jesus had to cast himself upon the dependability of God: we see the results in the given record about him. Responsible discipleship means that we also accept ourselves within God's will—and handle ourselves as men under God's trust.

The Preacher as Christian

The church rightly expects those who preach to do so as believers. The church also expects those who preach to so walk with Jesus that his qualities will increasingly show themselves in his

A Responsible Self

spokesmen, and that those qualities will be deep-seated and influential. There is in true Christian experience a direct line of relationship with Christ: his life supports, shapes, and serves the believer, giving a sense of difference and newness in the midst of personal history. Christian experience permits life on the level of a "real person," to use Harry Emerson Fosdick's descriptive words. "A real person," Fosdick has explained, "achieves a high degree of unity within himself."[8] His several selves stand unified on an ethically high level, blessed by a new pattern, and governed by a new Spirit. It is rightfully expected that the preacher be one such real person. As for the preacher in particular, God has willed to use his moods, his disturbances, his limitations, his crises, his sense of inadequacy, his vulnerability, and realized needs in such a way that the preacher becomes an example to others of what faith in Christ can effect.

Christian preaching presupposes a depth of involvement between the preacher and Christ. It represents a submission to Christ's demands. It reflects bequeathments from Christ for the business of living and serving. Thus preaching is done with a flavor granted by real experience. He who would preach must be a responsible person, a self that is subject to Christ and his Word, open to his purposes and vast power, and he should progressively show in his own humanity what Jesus made evident in his humanity. To do this the preacher must be disciplined and mind himself.

The business of "minding oneself" is given due treatment in the New Testament. Paul urged Timothy to "aim at righteousness, godliness, faith, love, steadfastness, gentleness" (1 Tim. 6:11), to keep himself "unstained and free from reproach" (6:14), to "guard what has been entrusted to you" (6:20)—meaning his commission from Christ, his message, his life, and those he led. As for himself, Paul confessed with proper pride the discipline by which he daily lived: "I pommel my body [*soma,* the self] and subdue it, lest after preaching to others I myself should be disqualified" (1 Cor. 9:27). Paul knew that if his life opposed what he preached he would have already lost the right to preach it.

THE RESPONSIBLE PULPIT

On Knowing Christ

How strange and inexcusable that this Jesus Christ who has so concerned himself with us should receive such scant attention from us! We receive newness of life through him; we meet God in peace through him; we derive hope for living through him; and yet, though we be deeply versed in the materials *about* Jesus, all too few of us have the sense of real relation with him. There is no wonder, then, that so many ministers are but mere artisans of the preaching craft, speaking aptly, but without "a life to back it up" while some others are mere crusading activists doing essential deeds but lacking the redemptive word. Giving themselves to what they feel as *their* place and role and prowess, such artisans and architects do not make known the full purpose of Christ, and they miss the needed substance of his life for daily life.

Paul once confessed, "I know whom I have believed and I am sure that he is able to guard until that Day what has been entrusted to me" (2 Tim. 1:12). Paul knew Christ. While still in Hartford, Connecticut, where he pastored a community that knew him well, Horace Bushnell once stated, "I know Jesus Christ better than any man in Hartford." Harold L. Bosley, who tells of this, comments, "But, amazing as it is, Bushnell is not alone in holding it. Most of the great Christian leaders through the ages have felt exactly as he did."⁹ Like Paul, such men had opened themselves to the big realm of faith, moving increasingly from a knowledge about Jesus to an acquaintance with him.

Jesus Christ is not best known as someone to be *remembered,* as if memory is the power by which he is brought before us. Christ is not a leftover hope, however persistent, but a living, companioning Person. He is not dead, lost forever in the "pastness of the past," but he lives on in a full and final manner—and he apprehends us. It is this that comes home to us in the deepest study of the Acts of the Apostles. It is this penetrating fact that faces us whenever we read of the boldness of the first believers. They were sure of his presence. They understood their role in his purpose.

A Responsible Self

They had invested themselves in his understood work. He was beyond them, yet with them. They did not have to recapture him because time had not cheated them of his life. Those believers sensed his presence with all seriousness and he revealed himself continually to them as they lived to his honor. There was no professional spirit to bind their lives or block their sense of vocation by his Spirit. Their allegiance to Christ went beyond the demands of the group to which they belonged, hence their sense of orders and directions for service was linked particularly to him as Lord. Those leaders recognized Jesus in that high place, and they regarded themselves as servants "for Jesus' sake." They knew two realms of being and moved between those realms with ready faith and discipline. The Acts of the Apostles shows us believing preachers who were responsible selves.

The preacher must know two realms of being and must move between them at all times. The preacher must combine two orders within his own experience and ministry. One order is that all-so-visible side of humanity, while the other is that all-so-hidden spiritual order that our secular culture and conditioning profess not to need. The situation of the human demands a sense of the holy. The preacher must be able to receive from both directions at once, seeing and serving with relation to both.

Some years ago when Andrew W. Blackwood published his book about *The Growing Minister,* he confessed, "Among all the books I have written for ministers this one cost me most."[10] Understandably: Blackwood had to write remembering his humanity as never before. He wrote moving, as a now much older man, between two realms of being as he discussed the preacher's work as the highest, hardest, holiest, and happiest in the world.[11] Blackwood knew that the preacher's work is what it is because Jesus Christ is who he is.

The New Testament teaches that true faith in Christ grants the believing person a relation with him, making a Christian experience possible and real. Certitude results, along with what might be called a Christian consciousness, which is itself an assurance of his influence and presence. There are always new distinctives for ex-

THE RESPONSIBLE PULPIT

perience where Christ is known and followed in faith. As a Christian, the preacher will not only be expected to believe and declare the teachings of Jesus, but also to show the particularity and power of Christ in his living, having experienced in responsible faith the reality to which the teachings point. All knowing is an apprehension of reality, a possession of or union with the reality, an understanding of its meaning, and a personal response to it. To "know" really means to perceive with an understanding true to the object or reality experienced. The knowledge of Christ is nothing less. He is the *object* of our faith: and the report about him cannot by its very nature be detached from his person and his purpose. The very report is the revelation about him, and from him. The faith-reception of the message about him is a response to Christ himself. The result is a faith knowledge, but it is a definite knowing, for life.

There is indeed vast range and intricacy to the relationship between Christ and the self. *His* life provides that range, matching and handling the intricacy grounded in our humanity. The relationship between Christ and our selfhood is better experienced than it is explained. It is a living relationship; and *life* does not yield to final explanation.

Paul discussed the knowledge of Christ as an experience of participation, a continuous sharing in full, with more depth and detail ever beckoning. This is certainly clear from those words in Philippians 3:10, "that I may know [*gnonai*] him and the power of his resurrection, and may share his sufferings, becoming like him in his death." The use of the aorist infinitive of the verb to know, and with ingressive meaning, emphasizes the fact that Paul looked upon the knowledge he had of Christ as not yet full enough: a condition had been established, an experience begun, but there was still more to issue from it. His word describes both quest and find, for Paul wrote as a believer "transfused with certitude," to use John Baillie's phrase.[12]

Karl Barth once explained, "Christ is that infinitely wondrous event which compels a person, so far as he experiences and com-

A Responsible Self

prehends this event, to be necessarily, profoundly, wholly, and irrevocably astonished."[13] Paul had the point of this in mind when he wrote about the "surpassing worth (*huperechon*) of knowing Christ Jesus my Lord" (Phil. 3:8). The knowledge of Christ is excellent, and it is so experienced, rising above and standing over us at all times. "In particular," James S. Stewart charges, "let the Christian preacher, the herald of the good news of God, think of his own life being interpenetrated with the very life of Jesus."[14]

No man's work can rise higher than the quality of his life or the lift of his faith. The experience of George W. Truett in this regard has been of helpful guidance to many leaders. While on a hunting trip his gun accidentally discharged and wounded his friend, who was a member of Truett's church and chief of Dallas, Texas, city police force. Although he was expected to recover from the accidental wound, the friend died. Truett lived in despair for days afterward; he even despaired of ever preaching again. His wife offered timely encouragement, reminding him of the grace and guidance of God. Truett tried to keep open to God; a favorite Scripture verse, Psalm 31:15, stayed on his lips. And one night it happened: According to his biographer it was a night of vision: "He heard the Master saying to him, 'Be not afraid, You are my man from now on.'" The next day was Sunday, and Truett dared to stand and preach as before; but it was not as before, because he now had a power in his life that he had not known before. The next fifty years of Truett's ministry were proof that his faith had been lifted and his life renewed.[15] He could preach more responsibly, assured that he had been sent and that he was being aided by the Sender.

Call and Commitment

One common element, among others, among the noted apostles, the early preachers, and those who have served him as preachers since is the direct *call* of Christ to so serve him. The same Lord initiated each call to this responsibility. A second common element

THE RESPONSIBLE PULPIT

among these who have served is the awareness of having been *sent* by him to serve.

The awareness of being sent by Christ also sheds some light upon the matter of ministerial succession as it appears in the New Testament. The records there lead us to think beyond the church as the origin of ministry. The preaching ministry is dependent upon Christ's callings to men. It is Christ who grants gifts for this task. The church obeys its Lord when it recognizes a Christ-granted *charisma* and responds in openness to the work of the person so endowed. The gift of preaching ministry is not *from* the church, but *for* it and through it. It is true that *consideration* of the preaching ministry as a lifework can begin from any one of innumerable promptings—some observed need to which one seems drawn, the influence of some godly preacher, an alert assessment of one's personal aptitude and "leanings," to name but a few; but the call itself, that sense of being "tapped on the shoulder," as Peter Marshall described it,[16] involves something more than consideration. The call to preach involves a sense of constraint: it involves an inner state of realization—when the field of consciousness has narrowed, an attitude excited, the sense of self touched in a most personal way, and a provocative claim made upon oneself to become available to this God-directed end. The awareness of a call to preach makes a man feel pinched by destiny. It is a time of private appeal. The ego is summoned and the private self is sifted on all its levels of aspiration. There is a sense of having been claimed, a feeling of necessity and a reason for being. The church does not tell a man he is a Christian; the man tells the church. The church does not tell a man that he is called to preach; the called man declares this claim to the church. When he has been conditioned and sent, the man's life will reflect that claim. And so should his preaching.

Catherine Marshall tells how the preaching of Peter Marshall affected her during her student days. "When I was a college girl in Atlanta, Peter first caught my attention by the recurring note in his preaching of conviction based on personal experience. In

A Responsible Self

a hundred different ways he said, 'I know this is so, because I have experienced it.' " She added, "To us college girls, the surety of his conviction and firsthand faith were more fresh and more impressive than any preaching we had ever heard."[17] Peter Marshall's work had more than the stamp of native ability. There was the unmistakable stamp of a recognized call from "the Chief." The ministry of preaching is more than a mere human choice. It is a response, a faith-response to His authoritative summons to so serve. So Paul wrote, "I thank him who has given me strength for this [entrustment with the Gospel], Christ Jesus our Lord, because he judged me faithful by appointing me to his service" (1 Tim. 1:12).

Responsibility and Relations

Every preacher who pastors will readily agree that there are peculiar problems that grow out of the preacher's relations within the household of faith. For instance, the preacher is involved in the life of some congregation, yet his relations cannot be as full along some lines as the members. For another instance: he is a product within the church, yet more than what the church is really capable of producing—so that some think he has some natural differences or spiritual immunities, that he is a kind of special breed, a guarded soul. But there are still other problems. His *charisma* and the institutional aspects that attend his church-governed roles might not always remain in essential balance. How responsible should he feel for the institutional demands added by the church to his traditional roles? (So many new roles have been added across the years that some ministers hardly feel ready for service equipped with only the traditional studies.) Nor is it unusual to hear or read about the conflicts that sometimes develop between churchgoers and their ministers. Doubtless, Henry Sloan Coffin was right when he suggested that "It is not his ministry that is of first importance," speaking of the preacher, "but the church's ministry in which he leads;"[18] but neither congregation

THE RESPONSIBLE PULPIT

nor minister are always clear on who must define and declare that ministry. These are but a few of the possible problems the preacher faces as he seeks to relate within the community of faith.

Or, consider the problem resulting from the massive network of contacts he must maintain. He must be able to deal with persons aplenty—and always. For this task he needs a considered openness. I speak of *considered* openness because not all contacts with persons are of the same order. There is an openness appropriate to a particular contact. There are the minister's contacts with the members of his church: they are intimates, after a fashion—the fashion of Christian fellowship, and yet his relationship as *leader* with followers forbids the kind of openness he would know with other leaders, his peers in service. The pastor, as shepherd, will want to stay close to his people, but this very service-role restricts him also as to the openness they can experience between them. As counselor he is restricted to deal with what his people bring to him concerning themselves; as educator he must be careful about telling what he does not know and to whom he turns to be advised or taught; as a man of faith he must take care in openly expressing any points of personal doubt. The preacher knows very well that he is involved, inextricably so, within what Charles Duell Kean has called "man's normality,"[19] which includes the horrors as well as the heights of felt humanity. But an indiscriminate voicing of his conflicts to those he serves can hinder his ministry. A "considered openness" means handling all his relations with selectivity in levels and ways of sharing. There are those to whom the preacher should be able to turn as his "confessional fellowship" when necessary. But openness to some mature, seasoned, understanding, godly brother in the ministry is of a different order and on a different level than the openness a leader exercises on personal matters with those in the church he serves.

Looking at the vast network of contacts that urban life demands, Harvey Cox has cautioned us to exercise more selectivity in private life to keep us fit for the demands of public life. He reasons that the breakdown of the private life unfits us to meet the demands of

A Responsible Self

public life. "Urban life demands that we treat most of the people we meet as persons—not as things, but not as intimates either."[20] Our contacts are not to be separated from our Christian commitment, to be sure; but Cox is right on this score, our responsibility precludes the erasure of lines of privacy. Jesus handled his network of human contacts with considered openness. There was a difference between the openness he exercised with Peter, James, and John, and that he permitted to the anonymous members of the crowds which followed him. He did not act with anonymity toward them, but neither did he invite them all to the fellowship known by the circle of twelve.

The preacher's life must be one of considered openness. A growing relationship with Christ helps so to condition him. So will a healthy balance of thought between self and others, and self and service. This balance is a must, lest one be beset by disabling self-thought, like Count Hermann Keyserling who said, "I want to live for all, and yet, more than any other man, I am taken up with myself."[21] As for the preacher, he is sometimes too self-conscious because he knows that he is constantly being watched and appraised. This can make any man apprehensive. James H. Robinson tells us in his autobiography about his apprehensiveness as a new pastor, young, inexperienced, heady. Robinson spent the first three months of his ministry in frustration every Sunday because he faced so many older people sitting before him as he stood to preach. Each face seemed to say to him, "Well, young man, what are you going to tell us this morning?"[22] He wanted to be approved; he wanted to have their favor, but he did not yet know the full value of being direct and simple in meeting their minds. Like so many others in the same situation, Robinson learned "the hard way," but he learned because he stayed open to learn.

Appraisals are sure to result, but a spirit of honest openness will help us to handle them and even shape them. Appraisals not only have to do with how we begin our ministry in a certain place, they have to do also with whether and how long we stay, and how we are remembered when we leave some scene of ministry. Every

THE RESPONSIBLE PULPIT

preacher wants to be remembered with high regard as he finishes his task and moves on to another field. He *will be* remembered: his strengths, his weaknesses, his productivity, his program, his attitudes as shown in his approach to problems and people. He will be remembered by the problems he solved or did not solve—and by the problems he created. An interesting report has lingered concerning Lloyd C. Douglas, the novelist, who was also an ordained pastor before he took to writing novels. Douglas is still remembered at First Congregational Church in Ann Arbor, Michigan, where he pastored for six years, because of his rigid rule of "closing the doors of his church promptly at 10:45 on Sunday mornings, barring all late-comers."[23] This practice angered the students, quite often late, who attended his church in that college town. He would have pointed to other things more noteworthy!

Every man has his proper gift, and time and place for using it. Some men have an aptness for administration; they can bring managerial techniques to bear upon church life, project plans, and dispense papers throughout committees and parish families, gathering all and influencing to a common task. Some others excel at delicate relations, counseling, sustaining, enabling men to stand on their feet when the winds of life blow hard and heavy against them. Some others will excel at preaching. But all will be appraised: by both people and Christ. The responsible preacher will stay related to both, serving as required, but he will seek honor only from the Christ who called and sent him forth.

Understanding the Black Preacher As Social Leader

While dealing with the matter of the preacher's responsibility and relations, it is necessary to discuss an obvious dilemma which the black Christian preacher in particular faces as a churchman in America. The very use of the word *black* or *Negro* suggests at once the problematic and emotional context of the dilemma.

It is no secret that for several centuries in American life the black preacher has had to provide a strong spiritual leadership

A Responsible Self

wedded to a strong social concern. In fact, the black preacher's appeal in religious matters has always been stronger and more effective when he has been openly and actively concerned with the social concerns of his people. The black preacher has had to speak and work *for* his people if he would speak *to* them. This has not only influenced the attitude of the black community toward the preacher; it has also influenced the black preacher's thought and stance as to the role(s) and responsibilities of the ministry. In a very definite manner, the black preacher's personal experience as a black man has influenced the determination of his church and public action. Whenever this fact is left out of the picture the black preacher's social activism during the present era of social change in America cannot be properly understood or realistically assessed.

The black preacher holds no passing acquaintance with the need for social equality; he has been involved as a victim in the very crises that clamor for solution. He talks seriously, not casually, about life because the involvement of his people precludes any casual approach to their human and social problems. He knows, for life has shown him, that human division has only meant desolation. He knows, for society mirrors it, that segregation is always deadly. The black preacher has not had to do research into the problems of living together; he can readily call attention to the troublesome history of this nation and give a pointed interpretation of the greater problems of life lived apart.[24] He has had occasional outbreaks of enthusiasm when legal decision scored a triumph for his people, and when the national authority has been exercised to uphold the laws that give their freedom integrity and support. Like the rest of his people, the black preacher has heard the stated fears and arguments against intermarriage, and the cry that the races are incompatible; but he also remembers the pictures of the ancestors of his people, whose faces on the walls of homes and schools betray the vast mixture in their blood, and he wonders why it is that some others who look at those pictured faces do not ever discuss openly how those faces came to look that way. The black preacher knows all of this and remembers it. But

THE RESPONSIBLE PULPIT

he knows more. He knows that real Christianity is involvement in the lives of those he serves—and at the point of their felt needs. He knows that he is under orders to *see* things as they are, *deal* with things as they are, and effect changes with concern for things as they ought to be in the will of God. His situation in life has nurtured this sensitivity, and his insights as a Christian have granted vision and been a spur to action. Like every Christ-commissioned preacher, the black Christian preacher has had to preach the gospel, but he has also had to work actively against the social forces that undermine human dignity and make the gospel seem only a wealth of words.

The involvement of white churchmen with them in social action during the sixties gave some hope to black preachers who had wondered why so few white Christians were available to battle against faulty racial patterns in the land. It was a time of jubilant hope when civil rights became a concern of top priority among white liberals. As church leaders, ministers, rabbis, and nuns swung into action in sit-ins, freedom rides, and other meaningful acts of confrontation, there was open evidence that a tough-minded commitment to fairness was at last on the agenda of persons other than black preachers and race leaders. (The tough-mindedness of those so involved needs no elaboration at this point because the roster of civil rights martyrs, white and black, stands in stark evidence.) It must not be forgotten, however, that such increased work toward fairness and social change assumed such strength and proportions largely because confidence was gained by a charismatic black preacher—Dr. Martin Luther King, Jr. Sounding the trumpet of conscience, and showing by his own sufferings a commitment to work for needed change, Dr. King's example helped to activate many who might not have otherwise so stirred themselves to act. Nor should it be forgotten or overlooked that the closest associates of Dr. King in his leadership role were also black preachers. It was something more than the mere fact that they were leaders in the black church that influenced these men to be socially active. These active preachers were men of sensitive conscience, men with a

A Responsible Self

stated concern for what is fair, moral, and legally right. These socially active preachers were leaders who knew the responsibility and the will to act.

The will to act has had many besetting foes within the wider church world. One foe against social action has been ignorance, a real lack of understanding of what the social problems *are* and what those problems *mean*. Black leaders have had to be quite vocal in the attempt properly to inform the ignorant—inform them from the inside of the problem, speaking as only the victims of social problems can see them.

Another foe against social action has been lack of courage: cowardice in the face of known demand. Social concerns in America could have been more effectively expedited much earlier in our national history if more responsible citizens and Christians had not lacked courage to promote them. Some acted cowardly because they feared being labeled radical. Some others were willingly imprisoned within the conservative concerns of the churches they served, cowardly in their concern to avoid controversy, crusading, and any activities usually deemed nonspiritual.

Some other churchmen failed to act in social concerns because their theological considerations forebade them. Some evangelicals criticized the social action of preachers as a secular deed, an adulteration of Christian work, an ungodly encroachment on time needed for the Christian's spiritual task, as a getting side-tracked from the main business of the gospel. To be sure, the Christian leaders and laymen must always be on guard lest they miss essentials of eternal dimension in their life in the world; but failure to see that the Christian ethic has social applications has brought about a widespread misunderstanding of the mandate of the gospel and has narrowed its concerns to the End-time alone. All along, however, the black preacher has been insisting that the secular aspects of life are moral at their center and that the concern for human rights and decent treatment is no side-issue but an understood implication of the biblical anthropology that declares every man as made "in the image of God." While it is true that a bibli-

THE RESPONSIBLE PULPIT

cally oriented evangelism is not to be confused with social structures or the promotion of a social philosophy as such, it is also true that a valid biblical evangelism does prod and urge Christians to press the claim of the lordship of Jesus Christ in the midst of social structures; and, further, it leads us to test every social philosophy for its understanding, use, and benefit for the life and affairs of men. Social existence has never been a side subject in the black church. The black Christian preachers have always preached about the biblical demand for just dealings with others. They have always sifted the Bible to lay out the stipulations about the duties owing between persons. The black preacher has always preached that the burden of the gospel is identifying love, and that love is always a socially oriented reality.

The will to be socially active has also been thwarted quite often by differences over methodology; that is, some persons have differed or been confused over just *how* the concerned person or group should be active. Boycotting, for instance, has had its defenders and its objectors within the church. Some have decried the use of this pressure-tactic, deeming it unchristian in style and effect. The same judgment has been spoken against forced confrontation. Confrontation involved *forcing* face-to-face meetings of men or groups with intent to bring out into the open evils that were previously submerged and protected by custom, tradition, or even law, so that others could see and react in the light of a now-enlightened conscience. Confrontation means "showdown situations," and it has been made possible through boycotts, marches, sit-ins, freedom rides, and other public protests and demonstrations. During the sixties, there were many church leaders, black and white, who condemned confrontation on philosophical, religious, and/or methodological grounds. Dr. Joseph H. Jackson was one such leader who spoke and wrote against the tactic. Jackson condemned confrontation as essentially non-Christian and divisive, adjudging it as a method that incites civil strife and bitterness—and as an essential threat to national order and process. Jackson has argued that "in the name of nonviolence steps have

A Responsible Self

been taken that led to violence; an atmosphere has been created out of which violence logically comes."[25] He dismissed the tactic of confrontation as an *ism,* part of a wider disruptive aggregate of protest methods he labels as "Confusionism."

There is no attempt being made here to outline or overlook the myriad problematic aspects of protest methods used in social action for change in our time. But it is of fundamental importance to suggest that an element of risk is always tied up with *any* method one uses in acting for what one knows and believes to be right and just. No social situation is ever altogether simple, but neither is it so complex that nothing can be done. The black Christian preacher has felt under pressure of need to clarify the issues as best he can, and to act as wisely and courageously as he knows. Social tension has been unavoidable; showdown has been necessary in many situations. He has had the will to act, to act on what he believes is the side of need, right, and the future. Through their positive deeds, the black preachers have prodded the public not only to watch but to react, think, and also reckon with the burning issues at hand. In so acting, the black preacher has dared to follow the way of risk, even parting company with those who for theological or methodological reasons reacted in disagreement or dismay.

It is one thing to disagree with the order of social battle, with the tools or instruments to be used, and the timing; but it is quite another thing altogether to act as if no battle has been necessary. Some active leaders have been moving step-by-step, making each advance a solid one, while other leaders have sought to move in a great forward lunge. Still others have wanted both church and nation to "stay put." We have needed reason and responsibility during this time of ferment and change. We have needed to be properly informed about the issues. We continue to need courage to act and methods approved by the concerns of the gospel. All considered, the black church continues to believe that right causes do not promote themselves, but have to be promoted; that right is possible when men dare to think right and plan right and act right; and that right changes will continue to elude us until we de-

THE RESPONSIBLE PULPIT

termine, in all Christian seriousness of self, that we will work for that right.

The tradition of social protest in America is not necessarily Christian in base nor in operation, but it is not antithetical to what Christians themselves should feel and plan when they escape provincialism and see the true implications of our task in this setting. One does not need to be influenced by well-outlined concepts of nonviolence to be peacemakers, for that is essentially Christian. One need not be a black man to be socially sensitive; that follows from living responsibly in a nation that is avowedly racist in spirit. One need not be an extremist to feel a burst of concern to act in the world; that is but compassion, and is essentially just. One need not be a brain in order to handle urgent questions responsibly; that is just a matter of good common sense and a regard for priorities. Jesus dealt with necessities and he dealt with them redemptively. Necessary actions are one matter, while how they are to be done is another matter. Jesus was always found acting against what was irrational and evil. He always promoted the will of God—taking risks to do so. The records we hold about him can teach us in our present circumstances of social questions and demand.

The black Christian preacher in America continues to take risks. He continues to face the dilemma American life has posed for him as a steward of the mysteries of God (see 1 Cor. 4:1). He must deal with the gospel and he must deal with the social implications of that good news. As a *Christian* leader the black preacher has wanted to contribute his share to the meaning, direction, dimension, unity, and significance of the ongoing life and work of the wider church in America; but, barred for so long because of his blackness, he has used his gifts to shape and develop a vital Black Church, working out his obedience to Christ in an enforced segregation system and social concern.

Roger Hazelton once wrote that "Some Christians have been philosophers, have had to be philosophers because of their Christianity."[26] Their situation made its demand. It has been likewise

A Responsible Self

with the black Christian preacher. It has been his responsibility to work out his own salvation and the social needs of those who by circumstance needed his help. It is reported of Hermias, ardent friend of Aristotle, that his last words were, "Tell my friends and companions that I have done nothing unworthy of philosophy." Aristotle, upon learning of Hermias' fate at the hands of the Persians, paid eager tribute to his friend.[27] Social action is not unworthy of Christianity—and those who have so used themselves in Christian witness shall not lose their reward.

The preacher is a man under divine trust. The church recognizes this stewardship of himself for the gospel when he is "ordained" to the ministry. The church rightly honors the preacher with its trust as he serves in his necessary role. The church rightly judges the preacher when he neglects his ordained functions. But the greater honor—or judgment—is from the Christ who issued his call and commission to serve. As for judgment: we must certainly expect it against self-directed efforts and the vanity of pleasing men—by cowardice, cunning, or compromise. The preacher is no casual or isolated workman: he is a commissioned man through whose work the church itself is either renewed or restricted. This concern needs more treatment in current literature on preaching and the pastoral task.

Martin Luther once wrote, "It is not we who can sustain the church, nor was it our forefathers, nor will it be our descendants. It was and is and will be the One who says, 'I am with you alway, even unto the end of the world'."[28] Yet Christ has willed to use preachers in that service, granting grace for the task. It is a trust that humbles and quickens the spirit, exacting dependence and obedient trust. Thomas Chalmers rightly prayed, "Let not a wrong humility or a wrong delicacy restrain me either from the testimony which it is mine to give, or the authority which it is mine to exercise. Keep me from the fear of man which is a snare."[29]

In 1938 a family of eleven fled from Nazi-controlled Austria.[30] The wife and mother was expecting a tenth child. One of the children, about six years old, discovered that her favorite toy had been

THE RESPONSIBLE PULPIT

left behind, and with that deep, hopeless, bottomless feeling of loss known only to children who miss a favorite toy, the child produced a wail that shook the hearts of both parents. There were no cookies or candy delights to use as pacifiers, so the alert mother used the ruse of a story. She made her promise good: telling about the flight of the Holy Family as refugees on their way to Egypt. She made the story modern though, even describing how the baby Jesus refused to make noise over toys he missed. The terror, fright, and sense of lostness all waned in the family as the mother lost herself in the storytelling, and the six-year-old child quieted in measured reverence and sensed adventure. All men are like that child—even Christian preachers: we are all but children to life, living always with some sense of needing more than we have at hand—and longing for that which gave us security at an earlier stage. It takes a Story to quiet us in understanding and reverence and trust. There is nothing like The Story, His Story, His life. It blesses our humanity, lights up our living, and gathers us up into the higher order of his purpose.

> Christ! I am Christ's! and let the name suffice you, Ay,
> for me too He greatly hath sufficed.[31]

NOTES

1. *The Adequate Man:* Studies in Philippians (London: Marshall Morgan, and Scott, 1958), p. 43.
2. See Oscar Cullmann, *The Christology of the New Testament* ("New Testament Library") (London: SCM Press Ltd., 1963), esp. pp. 76-79, 174-181, 216 ff. Trans. by S. C. Guthrie and C. A. M. Hall.
3. See A. M. Hunter, *Paul and His Predecessors* (London: 1940), p. 46. See also Ralph P. Martin, *An Early Christian Confession*: Philippians 2:5-11 *in Recent Interpretation* (London: Tyndale Press, 1960). *idem., Carmen Christi:* Philippians 2:5-11 in Recent Interpretation and in the Setting of Early Christian Worship (Cambridge: At the University Press, 1967).

A Responsible Self

4. Rudolf Bultmann, *Theology of the New Testament* (London: SCM Press Ltd., 1965 ed.), Vol. I, esp. pp. 175, 298-299. Trans. by Kendrick Grobel.

5. F. W. Beare, *A Commentary on the Epistle to the Philippians* ("Harper's New Testament Commentaries") (New York: Harper and Brothers, 1959), see pp. 75 ff.

6. See Joachim Jeremias, "Zu Phil. ii. 7: " '*Heauton Ekenosen,*' " *Novum Testamentum* 6, 1963, pp. 182-188; also Jeremias (with Walther Zimmerli), *The Servant of God* ("Studies in Biblical Theology" No. 20) (London: SCM Press Ltd., 1965 rev. ed.), p. 98, notes 445, where he asserts, "The use of Isaiah 53:12 shows that the expression *heauton ekenosen* implies the surrender of life, not the *kenosis* of the incarnation."

7. *Christ and Selfhood* (New York: Association Press, 1961), p. 42. The whole of Chapter II of Oates' book is pertinent to our discussion here.

8. Harry Emerson Fosdick, *On Being a Real Person* (New York: Harper and Brothers, 1943), p. 28.

9. See Harold L. Bosley, *On Final Ground* (New York: Harper and Brothers, 1946), p. 33.

10. *The Growing Minister:* His Opportunities and Obstacles (Nashville: Abingdon Press, 1960), p. 7.

11. *Ibid.,* see Chapter I, pp. 13-22.

12. *The Sense of the Presence of God:* Gifford Lectures, 1961-62 (London: Oxford University Press, 1962), see pp. 8, 12, 18.

13. *Evangelical Theology:* An Introduction (New York: Holt, Rinehart and Winston, 1963), p. 71. Trans. by Grover Foley.

14. *A Faith to Proclaim* (New York: Charles Scribner's Sons, 1953), p. 157.

15. Powhatan W. James, *George W. Truett:* A Biography (New York: Macmillan Co., 1945), see pp. 85-91.

16. See his *Mr. Jones, Meet the Master:* Sermons and Prayers by Peter Marshall, edited by Catherine Marshall (New York: Fleming H. Revell Co., 1950), sermon "The Tap on the Shoulder."

17. *Beyond Ourselves* (New York: McGraw-Hill Book Company, Inc., 1961), pp. xii and xiii, respectively.

18. *In a Day of Social Rebuilding* (New Haven: Yale University Press, 1918), pp. 157.

19. *Christian Faith and Pastoral Care* (London: S.P.C.K., 1961), see pp. 42-43.

20. Harvey Cox, *The Secular City:* Secularization and Urbanization in Theological Perspective (New York: Macmillan Co., 1965), see pp. 41-42.

21. *The World in the Making* (New York: Harcourt, Brace, and Co., 1927, p. 4.

22. *Adventurous Preaching:* The Lyman Beecher Lectures at Yale (Great Neck, N.Y.: Channel Press, 1956), p. 34.

THE RESPONSIBLE PULPIT

23. See John Cournos, Sybil Norton, *Famous Modern American Novelists* (New York: Dodd, Mead and Co., 1952), p. 22.

24. For an excellent essay on this matter, see Howard Thurman, *The Luminous Darkness:* A Personal Interpretation of the Anatomy of Segregation and the Ground of Hope (New York and Evanston: Harper and Row, 1965).

25. See his book, *Unholy Shadows and Freedom's Holy Light* (Nashville: Townsend Press, 1967), see esp. Chapters V-VIII. The quotation is from p. 178.

26. *Renewing the Mind:* An Essay in Christian Philosophy (New York: The Macmillan Company, 1949), p. 170.

27. Cited by Lynn Harold Hough, *Great Humanists* (Nashville: Abingdon-Cokesbury Press, 1952), p. 12.

28. *What Luther Says:* An Anthology, Edwald M. Plass, compiler (St. Louis: Concordia Publishing House, 1959), Vol. I, p. 283.

29. *Sabbath Scripture Readings,* edited by William Hanna (New York: Harper and Brothers, 1855), p. 5.

30. See Maria Augusta Trapp, *Yesterday, Today, and Forever* (Philadelphia: J. B. Lippincott Co., 1952), pp. 11-17).

31. Frederic W. H. Myers, from "Saint Paul." (page 1) Macmillan and Co., 1867.

Chapter III

THE SERMON
Responsible Hermeneutics

EDMUND P. CLOWNEY, citing J. van Andel, an old Dutch preacher, has reminded us that "the pulpit must not drive us to the text, but rather the text must drive us to the pulpit."[1] In the work of Christian preaching true effectiveness depends largely upon what stands *behind* and *within* what is said. In this chapter, attention is focused upon the hermeneutical "homework" that precedes preaching.

A soundly biblical sermon demands a valid hermeneutical base. It demands a "meeting" between the preacher and the Voice in the passage he examines; and it demands full meditation on the message from that Voice. Only thus does a sermon properly grow and take on maturity for its task.

A sermon is something more than a preacher's speech to his hearers; the sermon is also the preacher's response to what speaks livingly within him. Rudolf Bohren has rightly explained that, "preaching is meditation on exegesis . . . the sermon grows out of this criticism and meditation."[2] Roger Hazelton was treating the same point when he wrote, "This makes a sound and worthy sermon not alone the repetition of God's Word but response to it and reflection upon it."[3]

THE RESPONSIBLE PULPIT

Christian preaching demands responsible hermeneutics. Simply stated, *hermeneutics* has to do with the task and art of interpretation. It is that process by which the meanings of the biblical statements are discovered and brought over into contemporary forms and usages for our learning and use in life.

The hermeneutical aptness of the sermon will demand some *a priori* factors, some guiding principles, all of which will help the preacher explain, interpret, comment upon, clarify, and apply biblical meanings when he preaches. In fact, explanation, interpretation, commentary, and clarity are all activities subsumed within the meaning of the New Testament usages of the Greek word *Hermeneia* in its noun and verbal forms.[4] The hermeneutical aptness of the preacher is a must. He needs to preach with clear speech about what the Bible offers for faith and life. He needs to rightfully explain and interpret the ways of God with men. He needs to translate biblical language into contemporary statements of the perennial meaning of a text or passage. The preacher's homiletical task must rightfully follow this prior hermeneutical labor. Given the importance of this prior work on the part of the preacher, just what are the *a priori* factors which must be active for an apt hermeneutical endeavor?

1. As a first principle of guidance, the preacher must recognize that meaning is possible through his study of the Bible. The biblical texts were written with purpose; they are materials of signification. The biblical writings are not mere objects to be manipulated and arbitrarily handled. The words issued from living persons who took seriously the business of life as seen in the light of God. The preacher best examines the texts when he seeks to be confronted by the texts as living speech. In another context—but with the same essential thrust and concern, Martin Buber dealt with this kind of open response to written words, saying, and advising:

> . . . let him attempt, as well as he can, to take and receive the saying with his ears, that is, as though spoken by the speaker in his presence, *even spoken to him*. To do this

The Sermon: Hermeneutics

> he must turn with his whole being to the speaker (who is not to hand) of the saying (which is to hand). This means that he must adopt towards him who is both dead and living the attitude which I call the saying of *Thou*. If he succeeds (and of course his will and effort are not adequate for this, but he can undertake it again and again), he will hear a voice, perhaps only indistinctly at first, which is identical with the voice he hears coming to him from other genuine sayings of the same master. Now he will no longer be able to do what he could do so long as he treated the saying as an object—that is, he will not be able to separate out of the saying any content or rhythm: but he receives only the indivisible wholeness of something spoken.[5]

The writings of the Bible are purposive writings: they speak, and they must so be viewed as living words by those who interrogate them.

2. As a second principle, the preacher must recognize that he, as would-be interpreter, carries with him to his task certain prior notions, questions, interests, and a definite mind-set. Rudolf Bultmann has referred to this problem as the problem of presuppositions.[6] The interpreter should strive, therefore, to isolate his questions, his interests, and his presuppositions, so that they will not hinder his need for a fair investigation and "hearing" of the biblical materials. Only so can he remain true to biblical meanings and be free, for example, from the popular and pervasive cultural interpretations of the gospel and the sentimentalism of a secularized religious order.

Paul Scherer discussed this problem in penetrating style in one section of his last book *The Word God Sent*.[7] In illustrating how cultural interpretations infest our time, Scherer pointed to that inscription placed over so many public library doors: the words from Jesus, "You shall know the truth, and the truth shall make you free." The gates to our universities also hold that word! We all know, as Scherer pointed out, that most persons reading that inscription do not think of the original context of the saying, and those who preach also need to be reminded of the *if-then* back-

THE RESPONSIBLE PULPIT

ground that qualified the saying when Jesus gave it: "If you continue in my word, you are truly my disciples, and you will know the truth, and the truth will make you free" (John 8:32). In that Johannine account, "truth" has to do with what God has willed to do for man in Christ, while to "know" refers to the experience of radical openness and obedience as a disciple following his teacher-Lord; and being "free" involves the consequence of release from the bondage of self-life into the liberating will of obedient love. The proper interpretation of that saying, then, has nothing to do with a library, a university, or readings of various sorts, but rather with a man's relationship to God through obedient discipleship to Christ. Men who view that inscription invariably read it through culturally distorted eyes. Presuppositions blind the average reader when he sees those words over the library doors. As for the preacher in his study, he must set himself to make a fair investigation of the texts, and to have ears truly open to "hear" what the texts themselves have to say.

3. Thirdly, the preacher must consider the Bible as a "holy Book" that is, it is especially related to a special history and tradition which interconnect with deity, so that some special implicates attach to the study of it.[8] This whole matter keeps the preacher alert to the authenticity and authority of the Bible, and it keeps him mindful of the relation between tradition and truth. The status of the Bible must be considered in every attempt to interpret its content.

4. There is a fourth principal factor for responsible biblical interpretation: the Bible is a set of many books. The Bible did not emerge into history as a unitary composition; it is the direct result of two processes of compilation—and those two processes involved critical principles of selection.

5. A fifth general principle must be remembered: the materials of the biblical books reflect about eighteen centuries of history, many stages and levels of life, situations, and moral concerns. Exact study of the materials reminds the interpreter that he is dealing with statements, documents, codes, forms, and rules that under-

The Sermon: Hermeneutics

went development, were reworked in some explicit instances, and that these materials so often reflect a blend of history, conflation of concepts, and a change of audience and/or setting. The alert interpreter does not approach the Bible without giving attention to the handling its materials have been given in the process of being shaped in their present forms. The responsible interpreter is not one who holds an unthinking attitude toward the documents of the Bible.[9] He will, however, be guided by the fact that whatever the long and involved process behind its shape and cast, the Bible is basically unified in its message and concern—and it should be meaningfully described as a product of special revelation.[10]

6. The interpreter must recognize that biblical interpretation has itself had a long history, and that portions of that history can be traced in the very pages of the Bible itself. One matter can be used here to illustrate this principle, namely the intricate treatment across the Bible regarding the Sabbath law.

The basic statement of the Sabbath law occurs in Exodus 20:10 (Deuteronomy 5:14 is a parallel), and it is attributed to Moses. The command plainly prohibits work on that holy day. As time passed and circumstances multiplied, questions arose which made it necessary for the national leaders to categorize the meaning and extent of the *work* to which the original command should be understood to apply. The stipulations in the Shabbath (7:2) section of *The Mishnah*[11] show the rabbinic considerations that multiplied across the years as interpretations for handling the ancient law statement.

It is of interest that when Jesus reinterpreted that ancient law, he parted company with the many rabbinic considerations, and allowed exceptions to that Sabbath law on the basis of human needs. One does not read passages like Matthew 12:11, Luke 13:14f, 14:4, John 7:23, and Mark 2:27 without seeing that Jesus broke into the tradition of interpretation with a new principle. His freedom to do this, his authority in doing it, and his insight as seen in his explanation should be given their proper due in any study of the New Testament. Although he was formally considered as only a "layman," he dared to make differences and distinctions normally expected from formally trained rabbis. Jesus dared to take issue with a very learned group of men: they were men trained in the Torah, ordained biblical instructors qualified by years of formal study for their task. Held in high esteem by the populace, the scribes were usually subsidized for their role so that as a general rule they did not have to do other tasks for a means of support.[12] From all accounts, Jesus lacked their background and patronage; he was a carpenter by trade. Yet, in pitting his own judgment against the judgment of rabbinically trained scribes, Jesus had to know what he was doing. He dared his judgment because he was a hermeneut. He created a new tradition regarding the sacred day and this act marked Jesus as one who went directly to the textual passage to see what a fresh study of its claims would urge in the light of a basic human need. Jesus knew that fresh formulations were possible because he knew the true concerns of law and love in vital religion.

Jesus was a hermeneut who understood the living role of Scripture-wisdom and law. The men he trained followed his lead and made fresh formulations of how law was to apply in the Christian era. Going beyond dogma in a creative fashion, their handling of Old Testament "prophecies" is a revealing study: certain passages and statements from the prophets are sometimes expounded on the basis of a word held in common by those texts, or an event becomes a "fulfillment" by means of a principle of correlation or a typology. The many instances of proof-texting in Matthew's Gospel can be cited as evidence of this. Again and again the writer of that Gospel uses typology, the principle of correspondence, or recurrence, or reenactment—or recapitulation[13] to set forth some superior meaning of an event in his own time as over against an earlier occurrence in the nation's past. Or, moving over into the Epistles, one might cite Paul's use of allegory in Galatians 4:21-31 in his discussion of Sarah and Hagar. He also allegorized in 2 Corinthians 3:13-4:6 in discussing the veil Moses used over his face after his tryst with God on the mount. In passage after pas-

The Sermon: Hermeneutics

sage the New Testament writers appeal to their own day as the "fullness of time," as the point of history at which all previous events and meanings had converged. They read the Old Testament as reflecting the life and times of Jesus whom they knew as the Servant-Son, Christ, Savior, Lord. In all of these instances, and in many, many more, we see how the New Testament era persons used and interpreted the Old Testament era events and promises. Many lines of interpretative change and difference can be traced in these instances, but it is not the rationale behind any particular style of interpretation that is being highlighted here; the point is to show such wide and varied differences in the Bible itself of a history of interpretation. In preparing himself to preach on some biblical passage, the preacher-hermeneut must take note of this tradition—which might well have influenced the cast of the text before him.

7. There is a seventh factor to help the preacher-hermeneut of our day: He should use the positive insights from contemporary linguistic analysis.

Traditional hermeneutics has always given attention to the six general principles outlined above, and especial care has always been devoted to the grammar of biblical language—word order, mood, and technical terms. But in recent years a revolutionary thrust forward has been achieved in biblical study through the insights of linguistic analysis which have afforded us a new way of scrutinizing the biblical texts. Influenced by philosophy and modern historical criteria, alert students of language have interrogated the biblical "statements"[14] and literary genres with new questions. A kind of "new hermeneutic" has thus developed.[15] A more scientific approach to biblical statement is now in use, sifting that statement for its forms, the world-view of the writers, the historical background of the formulation, the basic reality of the phenomena reported, the historical meaning drawn by the writer from the event described, and the personal intention of the writer in producing his work. This is a problematic undertaking, admittedly, but it has been a necessary and honest demand placed upon critical thinkers

THE RESPONSIBLE PULPIT

because of new insights into human language itself, not to mention the built-in difficulties of describing or verifying the phenomena and meanings of religious experience.

The "new hermeneutic" uses a more critical historical method of interrogating biblical language than traditional hermeneutics ever did. Viewing language as an ontological derivation of reason, the "new hermeneutic" brings into question the theological presuppositions of the writer of the text. This more critical approach also seeks to get behind the language to the actual "history" or "event" or "experience" being recounted, and it tests the statement for adequacy, dimensions, content, character, and claims. The performative nature of the statement is thus studied, and the hermeneut can better know what to say about the text when he has really grasped what the text *does* by what it *says*. The new hermeneut is concerned both about the writer's concepts and about the context surrounding the writer's statement. The insights of linguistic analysis are of especial help to him at such a point of inquiry. Those insights help the hermeneut to isolate the biblical writer's modes and models; they also help him to detect the writer's "language-games."[16] This kind of study helps the hermeneut to appreciate the writer's particularity, and better grasp the particularity to which the writer points in witness or report. All of this is certainly involved in the hermeneutical task that is prior to preaching.

Biblical Scholarship

The preacher needs to know and understand the nature and terms of the biblical language if he is to deliver his message with freedom and effectiveness. Influenced by rich insights from modern linguistic analysis, he can go beyond mere word study as he sifts his text. He can go beyond the words and will understand something more than the writer's culture and theology, and even more than the immediate context within which a statement appears. The responsible hermeneut will also study the biblical writer's lan-

The Sermon: Hermeneutics

guage-games and how these influence the cast of his work.

Consider, for example, the following passage from Luke's Acts of the Apostles. The passage abounds in the language-game of mixed ways of speaking. The passage (Acts 9:1-31) is Luke's account of Paul's conversion experience.[17] Paul's vision of the risen Christ is being described. It was a time of unique encounter for Saul as he was halted while on mission persecuting Christians within the Jewish nation.

9:1. *empneon apeiles kai phonou*: "breathing out threatenings and murder." The present participle of *empneo* is here used figuratively.

9:3. *phos ek tou ouranou*: "a light from (out of) heaven." Is this ancient symbolism only, an expression peculiar to biblical literature to express in a figurative manner a divine happening? Or was this "light from (out of) heaven" literally observed by Paul? Is this textual statement to be understood as a straightforward description? The next verses of the account appear to suggest that Luke reports the event as both audibly and visibly real.

9:4. *peson epi ten gen*: "falling on the ground." These words are to be understood as straightforward description.

9:18. *(h)os lepides*: "as scales." This word occurs in the New Testament only in Acts. Is the meaning only that Paul has his sight restored, having been healed of his strange three-day blindness? Or did scaly crusts actually fall from Paul's eyes? Luke was a physician (see Col. 4:14): was he speaking figuratively here or was this a literal happening? Commentators differ on the interpretation that should apply here.

9:19. *enischusen*: "was strengthened." This use of the word (which occurs only in Luke's writings: Luke 22:43 and here) must be taken in its literal sense because it is connected with the result of nourishment after Paul had eaten. The use in 9:22, however, cannot be so understood as literal result because there *enedunamouto*—"increased in strength," refers to a spiritual strengthening. The use there is figurative in meaning and points to the intensification of Paul's spiritual ability as a persuasive witness to Christ.

THE RESPONSIBLE PULPIT

The passage bristles with mixed ways of speaking. Within the short compass of those closely worded sentences, Luke moves back and forth between literal and figurative expressions. He is plainly engaged in a "language-game," one of the many which were normative for the biblical writers. Concerned as they were about reporting divine action in history, and the meaning of that action for discernment, faith, and commitment, Luke and the other writers used language that often shows itself as "logically odd"[18] in its mixing of currency to performatively communicate. This "mixing" seems forced by the very nature of their concern. To be sure, there are always peculiar problems which attend positive reporting about religious phenomena.

The concern of modern man to know things with accuracy and fullness of detail can tempt even the preacher to wish that the biblical language had not been so mixed and "logically odd" or to wish that so many aspects that we consider important in true reporting or reacting had not been left out of the accounts. But the hermeneut must remember that we are asking some questions that the writers were not seeking to answer. Those writers were rather engaged in a task of witness. They were providing a foundation for discernment of God and commitment to him. They were seeking to convey meanings for faith and life. They had used the modes and models of their time. Our need is to bridge the gap between their modes and models and our modern ways of perceiving and reporting. It is here that some of the great questions of our time are presently concentrated. So Carl E. Braaten has stated, "The more sharply we put the historical question of meaning to the text, the more conscious we become of our distance from the intellectual world of the text."[19] Linguistic analysis has provided additional tools for bridging the gap of that evident distance between the ancient biblical-world thought and our own. If the preacher is not indifferent to these tools they can help him to apprehend meanings.

Lewis Carroll, in his *Through the Looking Glass,* pictures Alice being questioned as she found herself in a setting new to her:

The Sermon: Hermeneutics

Here the Red Queen began again. "Can you answer useful questions?" she said. "How is bread made?"

"I know that!" Alice cried eagerly. "You take some flour — — — —."

"Where do you pick the flower?" the White Queen asked. "In a garden or in the hedges?"

"Well, it isn't picked at all," Alice explained, "it's ground — — — —."

"How many acres of ground?" said the White Queen. "You musn't leave out so many things."[20]

Alice had answers true to her experience, although the interrogators seemed more conscious of the intellectual distance from their thought that her thought reflected. It does seem as if the biblical statements have left out so many things, but if we truly seek to hear what is being reported about spiritual life and meanings we will discover that in our effort to sift the text the text will sift and stir us. It was this that Gerhard Ebeling pointed out when he distinguished between the exposition *of* a text and being exposed *by* one.[21] "For the text is not there for its own sake," Ebeling has rightly explained, "but for the sake of the word-event which is the origin and also the future of the text."[22] It is for such a purpose that the preacher must become hermeneutically apt for his preaching task.

Preaching continues to hold importance as a vital act of traditioning and truth. It is by preaching that believing can occur. It is by preaching that Christ is heard anew. It is by preaching that Christian nurture is assisted.[23] Preaching provides for an active presence and a God-ordained means by which his business is transacted through a language- or word-event.

The Christian preacher must be concerned to do biblical preaching. Central to this result is prolonged exposure to the biblical statements and a faithful handling of the hermeneutical task. Some

THE RESPONSIBLE PULPIT

years ago when a new biographical study of his life was about to be published, Karl Barth was asked to read the study before the book was cast into print. He did, and he advised the admiring writer to make a few corrections here and there. Barth afterward wrote an appreciative letter to his admirer and confessed some embarrassment at being so praised by him. "But," he added, "if I close my ears to the 'overabundant praises,' I can assert here that you have understood my thought very well indeed, and that in your survey I have discovered to my joy the same intent which is at the foundation of my own life and work." A part of Barth's statement to that admiring biographer[24] is highly suggestive for the preacher who has taken his taxing hermeneutical task responsibly before his Lord: "You have understood my thought very well indeed." It is toward such an approving word from Christ that the preacher must be forever concerned to move—fully committed,

> Both heart and head—both
> active, both complete,
> And both in earnest.[25]

NOTES

1. *Preaching and Biblical Theology* (London: The Tyndale Press, 1962), p. 19.

2. *Preaching and Community* (Richmond: John Knox Press, 1965), p. 106. Trans. from the German by David E. Green.

3. *Christ and Ourselves:* A Clue to Christian Life Today (New York and Evanston: Harper and Row, 1965), p. 83.

4. See the excellent summary treatment on this subject by James M. Robinson, "Hermeneutic Since Barth," in *The New Hermeneutic,* edited by James M. Robinson and John B. Cobb, Jr., (New York and Evanston: Harper and Row, 1964), pp. 1-6 esp.

5. Martin Buber, *I and Thou* (New York: Charles Scribner's Sons, 1937), p. 128. Trans. by Ronald Gregor Smith. For one good study of Buber as an

The Sermon: Hermeneutics

interpreter of the Bible, see Nahum N. Glatzer, "Buber As An Interpreter of the Bible," in *The Philosophy of Martin Buber,* ed. by Paul A. Schlilpp and Maurice Friedman (London: Cambridge University Press, 1965), esp. pp. 362 ff.

6. See Rudolf Bultmann, *The Presence of Eternity:* History and Eschatology. The Gifford Lectures, 1955 (New York: Harper, 1957), p. 113 f.; *idem.*: "Is Exegesis without Presuppositions Possible?" in *Existence and Faith:* Shorter Writings of Rudolf Bultmann, ed. by Schubert M. Ogden (New York: Meridian Books, World Publishing Co., 1960), pp. 289-296.

7. (New York: Harper and Row, 1965), see esp. pp. 3-21.

8. On the concept of holy Book, see S.F.G. Brandon, "The Holy Book, the Holy Tradition and the Holy Ikon," in *Holy Book and Holy Tradition,* ed. F. F. Bruce and E. G. Rupp (Grand Rapids: Wm. B. Eerdmans Publishing Co., 1968), pp. 1-19.

9. See James Barr, *Old and New in Interpretation:* A Study of the Two Testaments (New York: Harper and Row, 1966), esp. the Appendix, pp. 201-206.

10. See Bernard Ramm, *Special Revelation and the Word of God* (Grand Rapids: Wm. B. Eerdmans Publishing Co., 1960), esp. pp. 161-187.

11. *The Mishnah:* Translated from the Hebrew with Introduction and Brief Explanatory Notes, by Herbert Danby (London: Oxford University Press, 1933), p. 106. The rabbis had finally settled upon thirty-nine categories of work to which the command would be considered as applicable.

12. See Joachim Jeremias, article on *grammateus,* in *Theological Dictionary of the New Testament,* Vol. I, ed. by G. Kittel, trans. by G. W. Bromiley (Grand Rapids: Wm. B. Eerdmans Publishing Co., 1964), pp. 740-742; *idem., Jerusalem in the Time of Jesus* (Philadelphia: Fortress Press, 1969), esp. pp. 112-113. Trans. from the German by F. H. and C. H. Cave. Further notes on the Scribes are listed on pp. 233-245. See also George Foote Moore, *Judaism:* in the First Three Centuries (Cambridge: Harvard University Press, 1946), Vol. I, pp. 9-16.

13. On this, see F. F. Bruce, "Scripture and Tradition in the New Testament," in Bruce and Rupp, eds., *op. cit.,* esp. pp. 83-84. See also Charles H. Dodd, *According to the Scriptures:* The Substructure of New Testament Theology (London: Collins, Fontana Books, 1965 edition), esp. pp. 28-110.

14. "Statement" here should be taken to mean the end result of the whole business of grammar, form, etc. On this see J. L. Austin, *How to Do Things With Words,* ed. by J. O. Urmson (New York: Oxford University Press, 1962), esp. pp. 1 ff.

15. See James M. Robinson, "Hermeneutics Since Barth," in Robinson and Cobb, eds., *op cit.,* esp. pp. 1-74.

16. On the "language-game" concept, see Ludwig Wittgenstein, *Philosophical Investigations* (New York: The Macmillan Co., 1953), esp. pp. 5e, 10e-13e. Trans. from the German by G.E.M. Anscombe.

17. This is one of three descriptive accounts as given by Luke in the Acts. See the other two accounts at 22:6-16; 26:12-18. Given Luke's carefulness about methodical research (Lk. 1:1-4), we can assume that Paul recounted the story to him for such use, but it is interesting to note that each account allows Luke to expand purposely on some aspect of the original conversion experience.

18. On this expression and its applicability to religious language, see Ian Ramsey, *Religious Language:* An Empirical Placing of Theological Phrases ("The Library of Philosophy and Theology") (London: SCM Press, Ltd., 1957), esp. pp. 37-40, 90-92.

19. *History and Hermeneutics* ("New Directions in Theology Today," Vol. II) (Philadelphia: The Westminster Press, 1966), p. 144.

20. Lewis Carroll, *Through the Looking Glass,* see Ch. IX.

21. *Theology and Proclamation:* Dialogue with Bultmann (Philadelphia: Fortress Press, 1966), p. 28. Trans. from the German by John Riches.

22. *Ibid.,* p. 28.

23. A most helpful study showing the implications of linguistic analysis for the religious educator (and preacher) is available in Randolph C. Miller's *The Language Gap and God:* Religious Language and Christian Education (Philadelphia: Pilgrim Press, 1970).

24. See George Casalis, *Portrait of Karl Barth* (Garden City, N.Y.,: Doubleday and Co., Inc., 1963), pp. v-vi for Barth's commendatory letter. Trans. by Robert McAfee Brown.

25. Elizabeth Barrett Browning, from *Aurora Leigh.*

Chapter IV

THE SERMON
Responsible Homiletics

HOMILETICS involves the preparation and delivery of a "homily," a discourse, a sermon. In the Christian preaching tradition the homily or sermon has been developed from the perspective of the Christian message, meaning that the aim and purpose of the sermon is to educate, edify, and enrich people in the faith. Across many centuries of church history Christian preachers have traditionally followed the classical canons of rhetoric in shaping the sermon—such canons as apply to invention, disposition, style, and delivery, but sermon *content* has usually been determined by the faith itself. Christian preaching may be characterized as partly commentary on some biblical text and meaning, commentary informed by exegetical study, and so logically outlined for hearing that the hearer gains understanding and inspiration for belief and action. The rhetorical elements used so to inform and persuade to action are: explanation, argument, illustration and application. Responsible preaching should be grounded upon hermeneutical insights but it is done with dependence upon homiletical skill.

The Christian preacher needs to have a ready grasp of the rules and forms and means for effective speech. He must know how to involve his hearers in the presentational immediacy of the spoken word. He should understand the basic procedures in sermon preparation, moving with surety from the conception and shaping

THE RESPONSIBLE PULPIT

of a theme to the outlining and organization of materials, and to planned ways of delivery. He should know and regard sermon logic, and he should be so focused as believer and spokesman that his preaching will show evidence of sermon life.

Sermon Logic

The logic of a sermon involves some "minute particulars." First and foremost is a well-determined aim and purpose. A biblical base is also imperative, so that the preacher's words stand rooted in the Word of God, indeed growing out of it. As for aim and purpose, the sermon is preached to offer a solution, or to instruct in a doctrine, or to effect a cure for some ill—personal or social, or to support a cause, or to sustain men and keep them on their feet while under pressure.

As for the sermon itself, it is the product of a mind and heart stirred by some human need, a challenging truth, a creative idea. As I have commented elsewhere on this: "Some germinal idea is presented to the mind in the midst of the minister's reading, counseling, visiting, prayer, or his 'coming and going.' A knowledge of congregational needs acts like a magnet and draws to itself known Scripture passages that clarify or promise conclusions to problems. Remembering problems of individual members provokes thought toward sermons. Some areas of truth always need to be expounded. Doctrines present themselves to be taught. The mighty acts of God need to be proclaimed. Goals need to be kept before the church. Christians need to grow—and in all dimensions. Sinners need to be converted. All these, and more besides, affect the situation in which a sermon-idea begins its growth."[1]

The idea arrives. The preacher views it and reacts to it with interest, insight, feeling, imagination, and finally, commitment. The idea does not come usually in well-ordered arrangement for easy handling. Structuring the idea for effective presentation might well take days; the process might even take weeks and months. Even after the first structuring of an outline, there is often the need to

The Sermon: Homiletics

work further over it, rearranging for sake of unity, order, and proportion. The time needed to move from initial idea to a ripened sermon can vary from sermon to sermon.

A sermon idea is better handled if the preacher can label or name it. The choice of a theme or subject is sometimes the first step to an adequate outline and sermon form. "The first requirement for a good novel," writes Thomas H. Uzzell, "is a good subject."[2] The same is often true for a sermon. The subject becomes a kind of peg upon which related and supporting matter tend to naturally hang. The subject and outline help the preacher to determine the range of his consideration in the sermon. As for the subject, it should be so worded that it becomes a promise of what will be said. It should suggest the path the preacher and hearer will be traveling. It should be so interestingly framed that it will excite the hearer to want to make the journey.

A subject is a guide as well as a name. It can be drawn from the chosen text or it can be calculated to lead the hearer into the text. At any rate, the power of a sermon is not in its topic but the treatment of truth. Having come to his Bible from life, or having first delved into his Bible for the sake of living need, the preacher chooses his text. If he has decided upon his subject first, he seeks a text suited to the need he will address. Sometimes in choosing the biblical passage first, the preacher can draw both subject and structure from it. Whatever process of selection is followed, the greater task is that of digging into the biblical materials for their proper yield. I say "digging," because it is literally this that the preacher must do: he must *dig,* going beneath the surface of print, using all of the available tools for study—original language(s) and/or worthy translations and versions; lexicons which clarify words and open to view the shades of emphasis which lurk within them; concordances which show both related and remote references; dictionaries and encyclopedias; commentaries and essential single studies on his textual materials. Digging helps a man stay informed and up-to-date, aware of previous handling of his subject and materials, and tested as to the wisdom or unwisdom of his

THE RESPONSIBLE PULPIT

intended use of them. When an original idea has stood the test of the digging process, it is usually worthy of claiming further time for development. Most preachers will confess that they have sometimes scrapped an idea when their alert digging made that idea appear inept, unscriptural, and unwholesome for use.

The choice of subject, text, and outline provides the essential province for sermon development. Within that trinity of details a way must be mapped to wed content and color, structure and simplicity, scripture and reason, stress and balance. Imagination must do its worthy work, helping the preacher to see the skeletal matters in the form of a living sermon. This means that the preacher must take time to see into his materials and beyond them. Imagination is very important because preaching does not deal so much with externals as with internal. Imagination helps to sensitize the preacher's spirit, guiding him, as the late Jesse Jai McNeil has reminded us, to "dress [biblical doctrines and concepts] in clothes suitable for a proper introduction to persons whom they should impress upon their first meeting and whose commitment they are to gain."[3] Imagination helps a man get a good grasp of the whole business before him: text and structure, aim and means, truth and hearers. G. Campbell Morgan confessed that he never dared to preach on any passage until he had read it at least fifty times—this granting time and occasion for sufficient familiarity and imaginative handling.

I picked up a magazine one morning, intent to read the feature article (for which I had made the purchase). The cover held my interest for a moment, and I took note of some artist's conception of a football game in process. The cover picture was a close-up of a crowded stadium. Something out on the field had everyone astir, on their feet. Wild joy was evident in the expressions on so many faces; it was evident that one of the teams had scored a touchdown. The artist had added a touch of humor—perhaps the central point of the whole picture: a fan, an "ivy-leaguer," was trying to return to his section after buying some pop and sandwiches for his gang. With his hands and arms full he was straining

The Sermon: Homiletics

his neck to see what the commotion was all about, and what had happened while he was away. He was disturbed because he couldn't see—his way and view blocked by the standing crowd. I looked again at some of the faces across the picture. His expression differed so greatly from the rest. The longer I looked the more lifeless their expressions became. I had felt the pull of the scene because of its suggestive details. Then I lost the sense of its movement as I—an amateur artist—began to study every detail minutely. I took hold of myself again and gave my imagination free reign. The sense of life and wholeness and movement returned only when I did that, considering the details in context. Seeing the matter whole, I got the intended impact again. That is what imagination helps us to do with the details for a sermon: see them whole and speak about them with a sense of wholeness. It is this that gives color to what we set before the ears of our hearers. We enable them to *see* with us what they are hearing from us. Apart from this, many biblical details will remain obscure for the people. Thomas Mann has lamented what he called the "laconic terseness" of some of the biblical accounts, saying that we see them in their bare, direct, and brief substance. His lament was that the "briefness and curtness . . . does so little justice to life's bitter circumstanciality," that the brevity and compression do harm to the truth of what really happened "as life first told it."[4] So wrote a novelist, whose enterprise of life was to *show* a fuller scene by way of narration. For many biblical passages, especially the historical and biographical ones, the preacher must know how to show a fuller scene. Imagination helps him, and in a spirit of sanctified concern he can help his hearers to see, feel deeply, believe with fullness, and decisively act.

The creative process must not be rushed, lest proper germination of thought be thwarted. The sermon insight must be given to the subconscious mind, and left there in faith. If the idea is worthy, and if it has spoken to the heart, it can be trusted to return in time, bringing "seven more" facets of focus. Remembered readings and experiences will help to mature it, and even test it further. The

THE RESPONSIBLE PULPIT

subconscious mind does an excellent job when it is given time to do its work.

Basil Davenport read something in one of the dramatic stories of Stephen Vincent Benet that reminded him of a work he had read much earlier. The marks of resemblance were too acute to be purely coincidental. When Davenport asked Benet about this, that master replied that he did know the earlier writing quite well but that he had not consciously intended the resemblance. It happened that he had heard it during his school days, recited by an actor with whom it was a favorite. Benet commented, further, "the unconscious does queer things."[5] And so it does. (This is another reason why it is wise to keep study resources identified and to give credit to those one quotes.) The subconscious does queer things; it also does the right thing, provided it is given proper time and is prayerfully guided.

Swamped by so many demands upon his time and services, yet having to preach regularly, the pastor will be tempted at times to rush his sermon ideas. Under such pressure, he must watch himself and guard against premature sermons. Faced by a routine of preaching demands, he must also watch lest his efforts become numb and stultify in what might well be called "production-line" sermons. Let me illustrate what I mean.

During my first semester of college study I began working at one of the motor car plants in Detroit. The kind of job I had to do allowed a fifteen- to twenty-minute work rotation between a crew of four material handlers, especially during the winter, since we worked outside one of the buildings unloading rubber tires and wheel rims from boxcars. During the relief periods I would go inside the building to warm myself. I also watched the men at work at the assembly line: They rushed about, of necessity, hurriedly picking up parts, attaching them where necessary on the hanging chassis, tightening the parts securely, and then sighing in a relief-conversation with each other as the half-finished cars were moved farther down the line toward completion. It was all so mechanical. It was but a matter of routine. Repetition had

The Sermon: Homiletics

trained those workers in steadiness and system, but the rush of production bore no stamp of "the human touch." Sometimes sermon-making can be that way: Dateline operation, attention to picking and placing illustrations, tightening sentences like nuts and bolts, and pausing after the finished manuscript or notes like a production worker, chatting with brevity and anxiety with someone else—nervously aware that the next one will be along soon. A sermon must be made, to be sure; we must give it structure. But a sermon must also have "soul," personal flavor, maturity. Premature sermons should not be preached, however grand the initial idea, and however pressed the preacher might be for one to use. When the points are not clearly set, needed illustrations missing, and the materials not properly digested for creative handling, a man does a disservice to both his insight and his people; he excites disgust in men who would have otherwise experienced discovery. "Production-line" sermons must also be avoided.

Someone might ask, "Just when is a sermon ready?" The answer depends in part upon the sensitivity of a preacher to know what *should* be preached and *how* it should be preached. Every preacher must learn by experience just when the sermon is ready for use. Intensity of awareness can quite often make this clear. So can further reading, especially published sermons from preaching masters. Such reading can be a valuable exercise to test the maturity of one's own sermon. Novelist V. S. Pritchett once wrote that "Experience suggests that a writer is wise to avoid reading many novels when he is writing one himself."[6] He can thereby keep his own thought free and separate from that of others. This is good advice for a preacher as well. But after their thought has spent itself, both novelist and preacher are wise to check themselves and their work for balance by some other and more objective measure. Between one's own grasp of the principles of his art, and worthy models shaped by acknowledged masters in his field, some ineptness can be detected and canceled, while some excellencies can be underscored. A preacher is not hurt but helped by studying others, provided he reads to reflect and not to raid.

THE RESPONSIBLE PULPIT

The Preaching Plan

Since he has to preach regularly, the preacher-pastor should gird his work by some resourceful preaching plan. There are many plans—observance of the church year, sermon series (biographical, doctrinal, Christian life, expository, to mention but a few). Most pastors who hold a high view of Scripture would cast a strong vote for expository preaching as the most worthy and resourceful plan a preacher can adopt for his work. Robert J. McCracken has commented that "This should have pride of place."[7] Many reasons can be given for this. Expository preaching keeps the preacher anchored in Scripture as his primary sermon source. It keeps both preacher and people alert to biblical themes, concepts, teachings, and the person of Christ, helping preacher and people together to gain a better knowledge, understanding, and use of the Bible. Expository preaching grants a natural occasion for dealing with some issues and matters which would perhaps remain untouched if only topical preaching is done. Expository preaching helps the preacher to guard against one-sidedness and barrenness. It also permits the widest patterns of variation, all of them essentially biblical: exposition of a single verse, section, or book; scriptural events, doctrines, characters; word-studies, parables, chapter studies. By this plan the whole Bible is the preacher's province for preaching, even as it is his major province for study and devotional reading. So many outstanding preachers have used the expository method, giving this plan such pride of place, that one wonders whether the very method itself helped them to secure and hold their stature and form. Refusing what Halford E. Luccock called "alluring detours of novelty,"[8] such men kept Scripture life and meanings primary, giving themselves to the service of the Word. A variety of patterns can be clearly seen when their work is compared and studied in detail, but all the variety and individuality unite in witnessing that the historical, didactic, literary, and experiential elements of Scripture can be organized and sermonized to serve the proper ends of preaching.

The Sermon: Homiletics

The task of preaching regularly—and with essential variety, creativity, and balance—is real and quite demanding. George A. Buttrick states that "students for the ministry are appalled at the thought of all the sermons they must preach. Years hence, if they are honest men, they will be still more appalled at the thought of all the sermons they have preached."[9] And they will find pleasure or pain in remembering the kind of work they gave toward the shaping of those sermons and whether the sermon sources were worthy.

A friend of mine went through a sea of troubles some years ago when his marriage failed. While in Atlanta one day he took the occasion to talk with Dr. William Holmes Borders about his problem. Borders listened intently as the friend spoke openly and with emotion. "I am almost crazy at this point," he confessed. "I am broken inside. Someone must help me to mend my heart." Borders helped my friend with needed counsel and pointed prayer. The friend told me that he and Borders later met again and that that wise preacher, always alert to insights for sermons, confessed that the way he had spoken about his need had "sparked" him. The friend was now beyond the immediate terror of his divorce experience. Borders rejoiced with him, and then went on to tell him that he had recently preached on "The Mended Heart," using the friend's phrase as his springboard. Without betraying the young man's confidence, Borders had seen life and possibilities in that friend's description of his need. The descriptive words illumined the pathway of that preacher's mind and he laid hold upon them for sermonic use.

Sermon starters are all around us, always. All of life can serve to prod us. As Elizabeth Barrett Browning stated,

> . . . For Nature comes sometimes
> And says, "I am ambassador for God."[10]

This also is her word:

> . . . A wise man
> Can pluck a leaf, and find a lecture in it.[11]

THE RESPONSIBLE PULPIT

So the sermon will usually begin with some prodding instance in life. This begins the particularity of the sermon. "But," to again quote Buttrick, "If we begin with life we shall end with the Bible, for the Bible is omnific."[12] Life is best understood and handled through Scripture wisdom; it tells God's ways with man. This use of Scripture assures the power of the sermon.

It is to be prized when life so prods the open mind, when thoughts and insights for preaching rush fast within us leaving traces of glory that disclose and delight. It is a most welcome experience when ideas and illustrations so multiply to our interest that our skill must be that of catching rather than finding or fashioning them. It is a time of evident enlargement whenever we can say, during creative occasions, about thought:

> Ye crowd on me! 'Tis well!
> . . . Ye bring with you glad days and happy faces.[13]

Indeed it is so. It is always heartening to plan for a worship service when we are readied by insight, skilled sermonizing, and prayer, intent to effect real difference in the thinking and lives of our hearers for God. This does make the worshipers anticipate blessing—and accept it. Every captured, creative insight is for the alert preacher a prelude and promise for bounded hearts and enriched lives.

But alas, sermon making is not always so fresh an undertaking. There are times when one misses the signs. There are times when thought just does not rush and when insights do not multiply equal to the multiplied occasions which press upon us for service. This was the problem of the friend J. H. Jowett knew, who, walking home from his church on Sunday nights "would almost invariably say to a deacon, who accompanied him, and say it with shaking head and melancholy tones, 'Two more wanted; Two more.' "[14] Said Jowett of his minister-friend, "He had no barns, or, if he had, they were empty!"[15] The friend knew pain and barrenness. Old sermons were cold, however hot they burned when first preached.

The Sermon: Homiletics

To have repeated them was unwarranted and a betrayal of what was lacking. Others have known such pain and barrenness, and with every journey from the pulpit,

> The pain returns, the sad lament retraces
> Life's labyrinthine, erring course anew . . .
> Awe binds one fast; tear upon tear falls burning.[16]

Some distinctions are important at this point. There is barrenness and there is barrenness. There is that barrenness which is akin to the dryness which sometimes besets prayer. Preaching involves human labor, and one tires in any work. This barrenness, then, might well be the result of overwork, indicating the need for a time of refreshing. Tiredness can dull one's reasoning and cut short our reach. Creativity is not an easy issue when the whole self is indisposed. Such times are not only evident to the preacher himself but also to his people. Anyone who must steadily create has to pass through such a valley. Given the proper circumstances, rest and reassurance among them, most creators revive themselves and renew their work in due season. Sometimes the very strangeness of the barren time can serve to give the life its needed prod. As Henry Sloan Coffin once asserted in another connection, "It takes something like an eruption of emotion to break through the crust of the conventional and release the creative faculties of men's souls."[17] That is also one of the circumstances needed. The very barrenness digs to the depths of a man's life, touching the wellsprings of his enthusiasm. It becomes the needed pinch to prod a man on to his destiny.

But there is another kind of barrenness. It is what follows from misused observation, squandered time, unessential reading, lack of thinking toward talk, limited devotion, and being too much with the world for the wrong reasons. So much could be said about each of these problem areas, and even others not mentioned here. A small notebook, carried about at all times, can be used to preserve seed thoughts gathered during the day; and, for those who can work in this way, transferring such notes to a card file will put

THE RESPONSIBLE PULPIT

many into place for further thought and use. As for squandered time, a happy-go-lucky scheduling of one's available hours for study and meditation will never yield anything of either discipline or worth. A preacher must remain interested in study or he will not remain interesting to hear. Observation, study, speaking, these must be forever linked. As John Henry Jowett has put it, "If the study is a lounge the pulpit will be an impertinence."[18]

Preaching is aided immensely by daily conversation with the Bible. In fact, there are greater rewards for the preacher and his work when he does not let a day pass without some memorization work on some of its lines and passages. It is surprising how much of the Bible can be committed to memory in so short a time, even time beyond the walls of the study: moments "snatched" from stopping at traffic lights, waiting at train terminals and airports, during plane or train travel, not to mention a host of other possible and regular pauses during a day. The late Donald Grey Barnhouse decided he would make a thorough study of the Epistle to the Philippians; taking a verse a day, he memorized the entire epistle in 104 days. The pace was modest but it was definite and regular. Reciting to himself at every possible opportunity, Barnhouse found that memorization granted him a familiarity with that epistle that proved invaluable for his expository work.[19] However, since most of us must read in so many translations and versions, we must choose which one we will use for memorization, lest the process, begun in earnest, be hampered by near-constant shifts in terminology and style.

The question of memorization aside, the preacher must be convinced that the information on the pages of the Bible is of a particular character, that the Bible is a repository of revelation-truth, and that it is ordained "that the man of God may be complete, equipped for every good work" (2 Tim. 3:17). Our faith, personal enrichment, stability, and effectiveness are very dependent upon how open we are to The Book and its materials. And we must seek to know it, not in bits and fragments and isolated themes, but in sequential history and substantial form, its framework and

The Sermon: Homiletics

features, its chief personages, and its lessons for faith. All of this is determinative for preaching. All of this grants richness to sermon content. So the preacher is not driven to his text because of his pulpit demands; he is rather sent to his pulpit by what stirs him in the Word.

The preacher who searchingly studies his Bible will be acquainted with the dilemmas and difficulties it presents, but he will also know and share its decisiveness, its direction, and drama. When biblical truths hold and handle us, they will also help us in the felt task of sermon-making. As John H. Jowett once put it, "Texts will clamor for recognition, and your only trouble will be to find time to give them notice."[20] It is not so important that we mark our Bibles, but that the truth of the Bible makes us marked men. Acquainted with its truths and themes, we will have little difficulty with the individual texts which "will find us out as we go along,"[21] to again quote Jowett. Responsible sermons have their demands, one of which is that the preacher be under the mastery of the Word. "The quality which makes a reader master of the secret of books is primarily of the soul, and only secondarily of the mind; and to get the deepest and sweetest out of literature one must read with the heart. A book read with the mind only is skimmed; true reading involves the imagination and the feelings."[22] A sermon which grows out of that kind of engagement both lives and makes alive.

Sermon Life

Sermon life has to do with what can make a "happening" for the hearers. It has to do with the nature and ingredients of delivery.

It is not easy to deliver a sermon with effectiveness. Effective delivery is blessed or hindered by so many factors: mental state; body rest, or lack of it; audience concern and atmosphere; interrelationships in the service between leaders, choir, people, etc.; the preacher's grasp of the material in his notes or manuscript; a sense of openness to the occasion; a concern for excellence in presenta-

THE RESPONSIBLE PULPIT

tion; a sound understanding of the process of communication; an aptness for invention; a ready vocabulary; a sense of control while under the pressure of the speaking responsibility; a keen ear to hear oneself and a readiness to improve voice tone and verbal thrust; openness to the "flash" that lights up the mind unexpectedly; inward assurance about a divine call to speak the Word of God; a sense of commitment to be God's spokesman. All of these factors, and many others beside, have a distinct bearing upon the delivery of a sermon. All of these influence the tone, thrust, and life of the sermon.

A sermon involves a dynamic *giving* to another. The gift is worded reality. Sound, perception, and meaning link in purposed fashion in a living sermon. The sermon is indicative; it is a sign, a pointer, an ordained way of order and ordering. A sermon is meant to give, contribute, bestow. It is a way of bringing men into community with God and with each other. There are some conditions which govern the achievement, and it is to the consideration of those conditions that we now move.

1. *A sermon lives when it is preached as an act of worship.* Pushed to the pulpit by his text, experience, and purpose, the Christian preacher will be expected to make his homiletics honor Christ. He will be prepared to offer his sermon as an act of worship to spur and guide worship. Since the sermon is at best a declaration of the Word of God to men, it is addressed to help men, but it is also spoken to honor God. No sermon that fails to bless God can ever help men. The more fully a sermon is understood as part of the preacher's worship the more it will be understood as a product of the preacher's life and purpose.

This understanding of the sermon as an act of worship has served to make some preachers wary of publishing sermons. George Arthur Buttrick has admitted his misgivings about published sermons, nor do his misgivings grow out of any fear on his part that homiletical faults will be found in his work. When he finally yielded to repeated requests to have his Harvard Memorial Church sermons put in print, Buttrick gave a lament, writing in the

The Sermon: Homiletics

preface to that volume: "A sermon is an 'I-thou' transaction: the congregation 'makes' the sermon almost as much as the preacher makes it," adding that "a sermon is part of worship, is itself worship—the ascribing of worth to God, the celebration of all worthy life before the Unseen Eyes. Remove the prayer-worship, the brooding of the Spirit on the worshiping congregation, and how much of the sermon is left? A sermon is an 'offering' on an altar. Perhaps it ought to be ephemeral. Perhaps it ought to perish in that sabbath's sacrifice. Perhaps no man has the right to draw it back, saying, 'I want to print it.' As to that I do not know. I do know that misgivings about printing sermons is not easily erased."[23] The point is sufficiently clear. The misgivings are warranted. It takes an understanding of the worship settting in which the sermon was delivered to really understand that sermon. A sermon is an act of worship: it should confess faith, inspire faith, and sustain faith. This keeps homiletics confessional, Christian, and centered.

2. *The living sermon is identifiable in its thrust, addressed as it is to particular needs and concerns.* No responsible servant ever preaches just in general. Again Buttrick reminds us that "Preaching is specific: its language is particular, and it is addressed to a particular congregation."[24] Each sermon, however classified—textual, topical, expository, or life-situation—ought to have its specific angle of approach and object of concern. Particularity always makes a sermon vital. True preaching is never "in general." The man who preaches is a particular man—marked off by his call to do such work. The content of the gospel is specific, with Jesus Christ in his salvific role as its focus. The Word of God about Jesus is particular, distinguished as it is from all other words and their sources. The needs of men are specific; real, individual, and demanding. The moment of hearing is particular, pointed, but passing on its way. The setting is also specific. Responsible preaching is always specific. John Henry Jowett was talking about this when he said to those hearing his lectures at Yale, "Gentlemen, our messages must be related to life, to lives, and we must make everybody feel that our key fits the lock of his own private door."[25]

THE RESPONSIBLE PULPIT

3. *Preaching that lives will be done with a sense of partnership with God and Christ.* Preaching is plainly a work of prompted action for God and with him. The biblical writer had such in mind when he recalled the ministry of "those who preached the good news to you through the Holy Spirit sent from heaven" (1 Pet. 1:12). The use of *through* here plainly asserts the notion of partnership with God in such work. This partnership is one of essential agreement of will and word. It gives zest, courage, reason, resource, and readiness for the preaching task.

A sense of partnership with God helps us to believe that the speech situation can and will *reach* the listener, that it will touch the hearer's life as he knows it. Every listener brings with him to the listening situation a prior conditioning. He is a man of feeling, thought, action, needs, desires, hopes, relationships. He has certain "facts" in his consciousness: some of those "facts" are worthy, some others questionable, complex, and puzzling, and some are outrightly unworthy. The listener comes as an individual self, but he is also a social self. Preaching must touch him at both levels. Better yet, we must bring the whole man into what we speak, and we must so say it that the hearer will see himself as a whole in the listening act, and react with his whole self to the word of address. Much of this has to do, of course, with the psychology of our role as spokesmen. It also has to do with our authority. A sense of partnership with God deepens this effect in preaching.

Vital preaching occurs when we are assured that our words are used by God to disclose his purposes and voice his claims. Properly handled—through content, craft, and commitment—a sermon is a decisive instrument of truth and a means of grace. In preaching, the life that is in the meaning of the written Word is released into the speech situation. Ernst Fuchs has rightly said that: "The miracle of faith in the New Testament consists of the fact that faith 'is capable' of God's word; not simply that it can apprehend it, but also that it can say it."[26] When the preacher has first listened to the Word, and has remained open to its meaning, thrust, and demand, he is used by God to shape the time of hearing into an

The Sermon: Homiletics

experience of encounter. Jesus spoke of this: "He who hears you hears me . . ." (Luke 10:16a). The present tense of the Greek is most suggestive: *ho akouon humon emou akouei,* the one listening to you is hearing me.[27] This is a fundamental statement. The Gospel of John also documents this tradition with the words, "Truly, truly, I say to you, he who receives any one whom I send receives me . . ." (13:20a).[28] We report, state, express, describe, and urge. We press a claim, but it is the claim of God upon men, *in* and *through* the Word. We speak for him. Preaching is something more than a human operation; it is a human operation done in holy resolve, in the spirit of worship, by divine commissioning, and in partnership with God and Christ. Our words in preaching must be considered against this background. Our words are given life by the Word and the Spirit of Christ. Knowing what we are to speak, and why we must so speak it, our whole service in speech to men can be an operation and means of grace. Attention to the voice—pitch, pauses, volume, tone quality—is important but it is not central. The central matter is the given *vision* our words must give and bestow as active signs of God.

The words of Jesus, quoted above, highlight partnership with him as the source of sermon life. There is a line from Paul's letter to the Romans that deals with the same essential insight. In Romans 10:6ff., Paul appears to suggest that Christian preaching is done in honor of the real presence of Christ. The "word of faith" which is preached alerts the hearer to that presence. It intervenes, instructs, and involves the hearer in a Christward direction. Then at 10:14b Paul goes on to ask—and note the rendering here: "And how are they to believe in him of whom they have not heard?"[29] Although the entire verse is decidedly rhetorical in style, moving to a climax of stress upon the importance of the preacher's witness, it is pivotal in its suggestion that Christ himself is the one speaking through the one who preaches about him. Christian preaching presupposes Christ—not as mere historical figure but as present spokesman through his Spirit. Christ is at the very center of Christian preaching, working by means of his word to evidence himself

THE RESPONSIBLE PULPIT

to the hearer, intent to shape and sustain a new history for the hearer. The one who obediently handles that word about Christ and for him is one who carries the authority of his presence and is a commended speaking agent. Paul's statement is really at one with what Jesus said, quoted above, "the one listening to you is hearing me" (Luke 10:16a).

4. *The sermon that would live and make alive must be rooted in the Word of God.* The preaching that God approves will be of distinct content and focused concern. It will follow the lines set by God for our guidance in preaching.

Preaching should be rooted in the Word of God because what the Bible says is of far more importance than what we say apart from its message. The Word must be preached because it alone is "living and active, sharper than any two-edged sword, piercing to the division of soul and spirit, of joints and marrow, and discerning the thoughts and intentions of the heart" (Heb. 4:12). Only the Word of God can effect the purpose of preaching. The passage in Isaiah 55:10-12 speaks well on this point: "so shall my word be that goes forth from my mouth; it shall not return to me empty, but it shall accomplish that which I purpose, and prosper in the thing for which I sent it" (v. 11). Such a word helps the preacher to do his given work with conviction, and it encourages him to do his preaching with a certain assurance of some kind of result. Jesse Jai McNeil offered an alert comment on this. "The Word proclaimed in one form has its fruition in another."[30] "And what this harvest will be depends upon the soil or condition of heart upon which the Word falls." "Whether the Word is gladly received or roundly rejected, it is never proclaimed without purpose or effect. To be sure, the effect may be positive or negative. As a positive effect, the Word evokes a congenial and holy response from its hearers. The Word as a pronouncement of judgment upon the unresponsive heart is its negative effect. Thus the Word goes forth in hope and judgment, to redeem and reconcile, to warn and to condemn. It shall not return empty and spent to God from whom it has gone forth."[31] Preaching not only points out what is the

The Sermon: Homiletics

way of the Lord; it is the living expression, when rooted in the Word, of what goes forth from the mouth of God to the hearers through the preacher. This is the grandeur and greatness of preaching. And, alas, this is also its weightiness. The preacher speaks for God, having been sent by him. It is something more than mere theology that he handles. His work involves him in speaking to the deepest in man with a message from the depth of divine concern. The only way to guarantee life for his own words is to root them in the higher given Word.

This was pointed up to me quite forcibly in a story Gordon Cosby related to a group of us as we shared in a retreat with him at The Church of the Savior some years ago.[32] The story was from his wartime experiences, when he was chaplain for an airborne division during World War II. A few days after the Normandy invasion his regiment was to make an assault into the enemy lines. The set time was 2:00 A.M. The assignment was admittedly dangerous and the men knew that most if not all of them would be killed. That night Cosby visited with as many of the men as possible, climbing in and out of foxholes, unable, in the darkness, to even see the faces of the men with whom he spoke. As he dropped into one foxhole and made himself known, the voice of the occupying soldier sounded out, "I'm glad you're here. I wanted to talk to you. I have a premonition that I am going to die tonight—that I will meet God before the night is over, and I don't know him. I want you to talk to me about Him," the soldier pleaded. And he added, with utter seriousness, "Don't give me any stuff about philosophy or theology. I just want you to talk to me about God." Cosby reports that he had to pause in order to really center himself on the needed word for that man in that hour. He found it in his heart and spoke it sensitively to that soldier. The words were those from John 3:16. Cosby spoke swiftly, simply, and surely in that moment of truth. When he checked the casualty list the next morning he discovered that the young soldier had died in battle as he had feared. Cosby questioned himself: had his words helped or hindered that young man in his quest for God? Had he

THE RESPONSIBLE PULPIT

given that searching man the Word of God or something less? Cosby decided that he would be God's spokesman indeed, that he would never deal with "wordy stuff" in his ministry. He would make each sermon a time of encounter with God, each hearing occasion be for others a moment of truth.

It is true that the voice of the preacher is but a transient voice. But the truth he handles is the tremendous reality to which he surrenders his passing self. With his words rooted in the Word, such a man can initiate deep enthusiasms, point out plain paths of duty under God, excite hope, inspire and enervate faith, and inculcate disciplines and doctrines for the safeguard of mind and spirit. With firm confidence in that Word, the preacher can communicate the passion he knows and abide by positions that its guidance sets him to hold. The Word encourages the preacher to trust his work as something more than mere words. It urges the preacher *to* preach, and also guides him in *what* must fill his preaching. This keeps his preaching alive and each sermon a living issue from his soul.

Our concern is for responsible preaching, preaching done by divine origins and with real needs in view. This kind of preaching demands three things of the preacher. First, it demands a "meeting" between the preacher and the Voice in the text(s) he examines. As a preacher he must expose and expound meanings for life: he must therefore see the texts as something other than mere objects to be manipulated after thinking about them. The words of the texts issued from living persons who were dealing with real issues of life under God. The preacher best examines the texts when he lets those texts confront him as living words. He must regard the personal quality in the words and see himself as a respondent. We cannot truly preach in a responsible biblical fashion unless we are informed through the biblical materials. The biblical writers have given us the speech of God, a speech which is at once message, exhortation, instruction, wisdom, demand, and *life*. The preacher must know and be in touch with that life through a "meeting" with the Voice in the text.

The Sermon: Homiletics

Second, responsible biblical preaching calls for the preacher to meditate on what he hears from the Voice in the text. Meditation, as I mean it here, involves a kind of dialogical approach to the Bible. There is a sense in which the written text is fixed, unconditioned, given; but there is a living Voice in the text that makes it a word of life, a word that never dies but opens up a future for the responding hearer. God addresses the hearer through that word, bringing the hearer into community with him. The given word is for encounter. The preacher cannot study Scripture rightly as mere literature but as a way of life, as faith addressing faith. Meditation on that word with attentiveness—a meditation that goes beyond mere exegetic and linguistic concerns for phraseology or imagery—lets the truth and life of the word betray themselves. The result is conversation with the Bible, a dialogue with what is there, a responsible responding to what is being heard. Personal involvement thus results, an inward grappling occurs, a grappling accompanied by an attitude to so receive, so understand, and so appropriate the text that its truth and life will be influential even beyond the self to others as the preacher speaks. The responsible preacher first hears, then acknowledges the authenticity and authority of the Voice, appropriates the truth and life offered to him in the hearing, and then he moves on in preparation to declare that word for others.

The sermon, then, is something more than a homiletic product; it is a product of hearing, a work wrought by head and heart engaged by God. This is what Paul Tillich was referring to when he said that "no true prophet has ever prophesied voluntarily. It has been forced upon him by a Divine Voice to which he has not been able to close his ears."[33]

Responsible preaching demands that the preacher remain under the management of the Word he is sent to preach. A responsible spokesman does not manipulate the Word of God, he lives under its managing direction. Paul was referring to this in his own life when he wrote "We have renounced disgraceful, underhanded ways; we refuse to practice cunning or to tamper with God's word,

THE RESPONSIBLE PULPIT

but by the open statement of the truth we would commend ourselves to every man's conscience in the sight of God" (2 Cor. 4:2). He who seeks to be free from the management of the Word, he who seeks to manage and manipulate that Word, is one who ceases to respond properly to it. The result is an empty speaking about God, an exposure of self rather than an exposition of divine speech.

A man under management of the Word will be able to do his work, even under difficulty, with grace and spirit. There is a kind of preaching, so-called, that is spiritless. It lacks something. Usually in such cases it is the speaking man who lacks something—caring. Let me illustrate this. I remember my days as a young boy, when I was sometimes called upon to join with some of the other fellows to make up a team for an impromptu game of football. I never really cared for the game; afraid of breaking a finger or injuring an arm needed to execute technical passagework on the piano, which I was studying at the time. But as my school friends would continue to coax and plead, they usually won my consent when they confessed, "But we *need* you!" Even so, I played football reluctantly. I followed the rules and was active in the game, but with reserve. My heart was not in it. I was not committed to winning but to pleasing my friends—and taking care lest I injure an arm or hand. The game was no real engaging event because I did not fully share in the spirit of the game. I was only going through the motions but lacked deep motivation. The preacher who is under the management of the Word gains spirit for his work; the life in the Word gives him motivation, and it inspires him *to care*. Paul had this in mind when he confessed, "For necessity is laid upon me. Woe to me if I do not preach the gospel!" (1 Cor. 9:16b). Paul had the spirit to preach, and he so cared that he never quit preaching.[34]

That trinity of demands also helps us to deal relationally with those who are to hear us speak the word to them. They save us from preoccupation with mere sermonizing and keep us prodded for effective communication.

The Sermon: Homiletics

All of us know that there are times when a sermon fails properly to relate preacher and people, times when it stands out as a thing in and for itself, times when the sermon stands more as a product of the man and not a means of grace through hearing. There are more reasons than one for this failure. Sometimes, however, the main reason for the failure is that the preacher became too self-conscious and self-concerned, failing to lose himself in his work.

Martin Buber tells of spending the summer on his grandparents' estate while a boy of eleven, and of the delight he experienced in the company of the horses stabled there on the farm.[35] It deeply stirred young Martin to walk into the stable and gently stroke the neck of the dapple-grey horse with his trembling hand. He felt the life and warmth of the horse beneath his hand; he was moved in elemental fashion as he considered it all—especially pleased that the horse did not react to forbid this contact. But during one visit with the horse young Martin realized that he was *no longer so involved with the well-being of the horse* as he stroked him, but was more conscious of his hand as a stroking instrument. The whole event took a decided turn in his mind. The relationship was not as before; the sense of self-thought blocked the sense of togetherness. The meaning of this for a sermon is immediately understood: a sermon is for a relation, a meeting of minds and hearts, a way of conferral and encounter. A sermon is a means of initiating relationship between hearers and a spoken truth; it is something to be heard and heeded, a means of experience and appropriation. It gives language of life. It presents the spoken results of the preacher's surrender to the truth he has heard from the word he was given. A sermon is purposed to give direction, for people act by direction (or they should). When the preacher loses himself in his work of directing, giving, speaking, bestowing meaning, the sermon relates with the needs of the hearers. When the preacher becomes the victim of his own thought, trapped by self-concern as he speaks, communication is jeopardized and his relationship to his true purpose as spokesman is broken. A sermon in itself is not meant to *be* so much *as it is to do*.

THE RESPONSIBLE PULPIT

NOTES

1. James Earl Massey, *The Worshiping Church:* A Guide to the Experience of Worship (Anderson: Warner Press, 1961), pp. 68-69.
2. *The Technique of the Novel* (New York: J. B. Lippincott Co., 1947), p. 13.
3. *The Preacher—Prophet in Mass Society* (Grand Rapids: Wm. B. Eerdmans Publishing Co., 1961), p. 97.
4. See *Joseph in Egypt* (New York: Alfred A. Knopf, 1938), Volume 2, p. 370.
5. From a biographical preface to *Selected Works of Stephen Vincent Benet* (New York: Farrar and Rinehart, Inc., 1942), Volume One, Poetry, p. xiii.
6. *The Living Novel* (New York: Reynal and Hitchcock, 1947), p. 9.
7. *The Making of the Sermon* (New York: Harper and Brothers, 1956), p. 30.
8. *In the Minister's Workshop* (Nashville: Abingdon-Cokesbury Press, 1944) p. 148.
9. *Jesus Came Preaching:* Christian Preaching in the New Age (New York: Charles Scribner's Sons, 1931), p. 148.
10. From "Aurora Leigh," Book VII, lines 465-466.
11. *Ibid.,* lines 732-733.
12. Buttrick, *op. cit.,* p. 147.
13. From Goethe's Dedication to *Faust,* lines 5 and 9.
14. John H. Jowett, *The Preacher: His Life and Work* (New York: Harper and Brothers, 1912), p. 121.
15. *Ibid.,* p. 121.
16. From Goethe's Dedication to *Faust,* lines 13-14.
17. *In a Day of Social Rebuilding* (New Haven: Yale University Press, 1918), p. 78.
18. *Op. cit.,* p. 114.
19. "On Expository Preaching," *We Prepare and Preach:* The Practice of Sermon Construction and Delivery (Chicago: Moody Press, 1959), p. 32. Clarence S. Roddy, editor.
20. *Op. cit.,* p. 121.
21. *Ibid.,* p. 118.

The Sermon: Homiletics

22. Hamilton Wright Mabie, *My Study Fire:* Second Series (New York: Dodd, Mead and Company, 1894), pp. 2-3.
23. *Sermons Preached in a University Church* (Nashville: Abingdon Press, 1959), p. 9.
24. *Ibid.,* p. 7.
25. Jowett, *op. cit.,* p. 137.
26. *Studies of the Historical Jesus* ("Studies in Biblical Theology" No. 42) (London: SCM Press Ltd., 1964), p. 192.
27. Charles B. Williams translates, "Whoever listens to you listens to me." *The New Testament:* A Private Translation in the Language of the People (Chicago: Moody Press, 1953), p. 156. *The New English Bible,* N T, gives the same rendering.
28. See C. H. Dodd's lengthy discussion of the correspondence of this verse with the synoptic sayings in his work, *Historical Tradition in the Fourth Gospel* (Cambridge: At the University Press, 1963), pp. 345-347.
29. An excellent treatment of this passage appears in Henrik Ljungman's *Pistis:* A Study of Its Presuppositions and Its Meaning in Pauline Use (Lund: C.W.K. Gleerup, 1964), esp. pp. 87-102. A few modern renderings follow the line I have suggested in the translation given above, i.e., New American Standard Bible: New Testament, and William Beck's *New Testament in the Language of Today.*
30. McNeil, *op. cit.,* p. 105.
31. *Ibid.,* p. 106.
32. The statement has since appeared in Elizabeth's O'Connor's *Call to Commitment:* The Story of the Church of The Saviour, Washington, D.C. (New York: Evanston, and London: Harper and Row, Publishers, 1963), see pp. 11-12.
33. Paul Tillich, *The Shaking of the Foundations* (New York: Charles Scribner's Sons, 1948), p. 8.
34. For an excellent discussion of caring in relation to responsibility, see Herbert Fingarette, *On Responsibility* (New York: Basic Books, Inc., 1967), esp. pp. 33-38.
35. See Martin Buber, *Between Man and Man* (New York: The MacMillan Co.), p. 11.

Chapter V

CONTENT
Insights From the Preaching of Jesus

JESUS OF NAZARETH was a preacher par excellence. Again and again the gospel records show him at work addressing men, discoursing, guiding hearers in doctrine, discipline, and devotion.

Jesus lived and served at a time in the history of his people when the institution of preaching was highly extolled. It is not incidental that from the time of Moses down to Hillel the leaders were honored for their ability to be spokesmen as well as liturgists; it was a distinct honor to be referred to as a "preacher." Preaching was an honored action: it was speaking for God, speaking as a free and alert spokesman, a servant with a beneficial, directive, and ultimate word. If a man knew his Old Testament quite well and had a good grasp upon its meanings, if he could cultivate a popular approach to his hearers and, remain subject to the leadership of the synagogue, he could exercise his speaking gift and *charisma* with freedom and distinction, especially during Sabbath assemblies.[1]

The Gospel records show that Jesus was one such preacher. He gained a coveted following and reputation. He spoke in the syna-

THE RESPONSIBLE PULPIT

gogues on occasion but it appears that he exercised himself more so in speaking to men out in the open air, on the wide fields, on a hillside, or beside a lake shore.

The Sermon on the Mount locates Jesus in an open air scene, speaking to his hearers while on a hillside. It is the sermon of a free man, an informed, skilled, and insightful man. The Sermon shows us a resourceful preacher at work interpreting lengthy passages from the Old Testament in a fresh and vital fashion. The style of the Sermon is attractive and the applications of pointed statements are uniquely apt: even the "cold print" of Matthew's record lets us see that the preaching of Jesus was "fresh, earnest, useful, and devotional."[2] Nor do we miss the ringing note of his authority. Jesus did not preach with the reticence of one under orders of a patron-Rabbi, as was the case with some other spokesmen.[3] Jesus claimed full appointment by God himself. The crowds that heard him sensed the truth behind that claim and "were astonished at his teaching, for he taught them as one who had authority, and not as their scribes" (Matt. 7:28-29). Here, then, is the Sermon of the ages, a sermon of imposing dimensions, a sermon preached to make a difference in the hearers—and show what that difference means in the sight of God and men.

Characteristics of Jesus' Preaching

Note carefully, through this Sermon on the Mount, *the ability of Jesus to blend preaching and teaching.* This is no minor accomplishment. We tend to separate the two, underscoring the firm distinctions between them, saying that teaching is mostly concerned with the structure of beliefs while preaching seeks the attention of the hearer and his commitment.[4] Judging from the Sermon on the Mount, Jesus the preacher did not separate these activities but sought to blend them. In his attempts to win men, Jesus teachingly described the character of the life to which he summoned them. He instructed as he invited; he let his parables effectively preach the doctrines they illustrated. The late Donald M.

Content

Baillie told of addressing a group of preachers on the subject of how to preach Christian doctrine. During the lecture Baillie confessed regret that he had not made his previous pastoral ministry more distinctly one of teaching; he said that if he had to begin again he would give himself more to a teaching role in the pastorate. Baillie said all of this as one who had become a seminary professor. When he made the same admission to one of his divinity classes, one of the students asked whether his present work had not really influenced his thought about a teaching ministry. Baillie admitted the fairness of the question but went on to assure the student that he had really thought out the matter and truly felt that preaching should involve more teaching within itself.[5] Jesus knew that message and doctrine were fundamental content—and as such implied teaching. But he proclaimed as he taught. He made his teachings preach. The Sermon on the Mount is plainly instruction, as when he took his seat "and taught them" (5:2); but it is also preached invitation, as when he beckoned the hearers to "Enter by the narrow gate . . . that leads to life . . ." (7:13a, 14b).

Leschetizky the pianist told his boy student Artur Schnabel, "You will never be a pianist. You are a musician."[6] He said this to his student on more than one occasion, even in the presence of others. But that teacher was proven wrong in his judgment, because in later life Schnabel proved himself to be both musician and pianist. The adult Schnabel sometimes delighted in repeating his teacher's supposed prophecy because he wanted men to know that he made no distinction between being a pianist and being a musician. He knew that in his life both were fused, both were allies in his concern. Teaching and preaching are allies. They can serve in a useful blend. Jesus blended them, as this Sermon shows.

Dealing with Specifics

The Sermon on the Mount shows us that *Jesus the preacher did not deal with generalities but specifics in his preaching.* He dealt with what God labels as proper life for man. He dealt with the

THE RESPONSIBLE PULPIT

human situation, with how men mishandle themselves and mistreat each other, with the need of every man to break free from selfishness and live for God. He dealt with the consequences to men of selfish living and godly living. He restated the divine commands. He also spoke of divine love, and offered help for specific needs.

Jesus spoke with strong word and sure insight. He knew and lived by the known regulations of the Law. (We see his obedience to the Law in the Lucan story about the healing of the ten lepers [17:11-19]: once he healed them, Jesus instructed them to follow the legal means prescribed in Leviticus [13-14] as testimony to their changed fortune.) Jesus did not seek to repeal what was Law, but to show how best to regard it, understand it, and live out its demands. Law has always been the formal element in the encounter with God; it prescribes for human conduct in keeping with that encounter. So Jesus himself rightly dealt with specifics in this sermon. He preached from within the Law, opening its intent to view.

The revelation and commands from Sinai are in constant view in one large section of this sermon. Jesus knew, as did all the Jews, that the Sinai event was singular and salvific. There was both revelation and response, encounter and prescriptive word. Jesus handled the prescriptive word with authoritative bearing: his treatment shows that he saw the divine Law in perspective, and he was intent to examine and expose each command in its context for faith, life, and worship. His accent is unmistakable: "But I am saying to you." He preached as God's spokesman. He gave his word with authority and thus showed the supreme mark of the man who would bring the Messianic Age,[7] the one who would renew God's covenant with the people.[8] Jesus preached with strong word and sure insight. He dealt with specifics *of* life *for* life. He guided his hearers by an "inherent right and manifest capability."[9]

Focused on Relationships

The Sermon on the Mount makes it clear that *Jesus did not preach about doing alone, but also about being, and how the two*

Content

relate. This sermon illustrates that true righteousness which follows from decisive dedication of self to God. It is God who has defined what is "right," and the right is stated in terms of Law. This sermon is about what is right, but it shows more: it deals with right and righteousness. The one is a position, while the other is a quality of life. According to Jesus, a man does what he is, and he is what he does. If he is committed to God, he obeys him. If he does not obey, he is uncommitted, standing in the wrong, and unrighteous in heart. The Sermon on the Mount shows us the disciplines of the gospel. It encourages the hearer to follow the lines laid down by God for human life at its best. The fact is that a man must either be disciplined in the will of God or he will be deviant from God. The sermon warns that there is no middle ground between the two positions. God makes righteous the hearer who voluntarily consents to the disciplines of the gospel. The disciplined man lives because he follows the lines for realizing that life. Those lines do not make him righteous; they rather teach his spirit which stands committed to the will of God. The word at Matthew 7:17 is clearly put: "So, every sound tree bears good fruit, but the bad tree bears evil fruit."

The Sermon on the Mount shows us that *Jesus blended prophetic and pastoral elements in his preaching*. No one can miss the prophetic thrust of this sermon. Prophetic strength and urgency ring clear in that line from Jesus to his hearers, "But I am saying to you." The tone unmistakably recalls the prophetic tradition.[10] Add to this the numerous citations from Scripture, the extensive and profound handling of insights from Deuteronomy, and the stirring close of the sermon itself, which is a warning about what happens when his words are rejected, and we see that the blazing rhetoric is essentially akin to the prophetic models found in the Old Testament. Jesus preached with authority, and used it in its necessary functions; to upbraid, pronounce woes, utter convictions,

THE RESPONSIBLE PULPIT

and give decisive interpretations and demands. This was plainly prophetic. There is criticism in this sermon; criticism of narrow views of ritual and religion, social abuses, economic concerns, pride, class prejudices, religious snobbery, and affectation. There are criteria here for judging life at its best, ideals for testing the heart and its concerns, and principles for weighing motives and treating men. This sermon holds nothing theoretical or abstract. Prophetic preaching does not deal with the theoretical, it deals with truth, in context for human use in living. Prophetic preaching deals with life as a sacred trust, a gift of supreme value to be handled in sincerity, gratitude, faithfulness, and obedience. It deals with God and man: God's demands and his just dealings, man's hopes and needs. The prophet gives information, reasons for hope, emphases for balance, and a realistic understanding of issues. The Sermon on the Mount certainly contains mention of all of these. It holds a prophetic word spoken in prophetic style by one who preached like a prophet—"and more than a prophet."

Consider also the pastoral flavor in the Sermon. "Therefore I tell you, do not be anxious about your life . . ." (Matt. 6:25). These lines lift the heart. So do the Beatitudes. There is deep compassion here. There is pastoral counsel here. There are suggestive insights for the handling of situations, strains, self. Jesus preached with pastoral concern, exhorting to faith, lifting practical priorities to view, and showing the concern of God in his own openness to those who heard him. The preaching of Jesus blended prophetic power and pastoral concern.

The Sermon on the Mount is also *filled with evangelistic concern*. Jesus came preaching good news: good news about the rule of God, inward newness, the power of prayer, the quality of mercy, the experience of forgiveness, and a proper view of the self in the world. His preaching discussed powers greater than man: legitimate powers, illegitimate powers, divine powers, evil powers, powers that bind and powers that bless. Jesus preached to give men a vision of life under God, God as Father. That unique vision highlights evangelistic concern, God's desire and action to savingly in-

Content

volve man. As evangelist Jesus prodded his hearers to see this truth and embrace the hope it excites. His statements were so provocatively arranged as to make that vision clear and God's call unmistakably heard.

A Message for the World

It is fitting to conclude, then, by stating that *Jesus preached not only for the church but for the wider world as well.* Matthew's version explains that crowds were in attendance when the Sermon on the Mount was delivered. "Seeing the crowds" (5:1), he commented—reflecting upon the vast assembly of followers described at the end of Chapter 4 (v. 25), Jesus was constrained to speak. The circle of the Twelve were his primary listeners; they sat immediately in front of him. But the Twelve were only part of a wider audience that faced and listened to him. What Jesus preached belongs to a far wider circle than those who sit nearest to him. Some men are in a secondary place of hearing; they must become primary listeners and committed disciples.

Jesus preached as he lived, with concern in his heart for the whole world. The setting, substance, and spirit of the Sermon on the Mount forever remind us that this is so.

NOTES

1. See Alfred Edersheim, *The Life and Times of Jesus the Messiah,* Vol. 1 (New York: Longmans, Green, and Co., 1899), pp. 446 ff. In the time of Jesus a man did not have to hold a theological title or be ordained to preach to the populace. Later, however, in the second century AD, preaching became the exclusive privilege of titled men and scribes. See Joachim Jeremias, *New Testament Theology: The Proclamation of Jesus* (New York: Charles Scribner's Sons, 1971), p. 77. Trans. from the German by John Bowden.

2. *Ibid.,* p. 449.

THE RESPONSIBLE PULPIT

3. See *Ibid.,* esp. pp. 445, 449-450.

4. See, for example, Charles H. Dodd, *The Apostolic Preaching and Its Developments* (New York: Harper and Brothers, 1960 impression), pp. 7-8.

5. *Theology of the Sacraments:* and Other Papers (London: Faber and Faber, Ltd., 1964 edition), see pp. 141-142.

6. Artur Schnabel, *My Life and Music* (London: Longmans, Green and Co., Ltd., 1961), p. 11; see also "Artur Schnabel: A Tribute by Clifford Curzon," Cesar Saerchinger, *Artur Schnabel:* A Biography (New York: Bodd, Mead and Co., 1957), p. vii.

7. See Norman Perrin, *The Kingdom of God in the Teaching of Jesus* (London: SCM Press, Ltd., 1963), esp, pp. 76-78.

8. On this, see D. Barthelemy and J. T. Milik, *Discoveries in the Judean Desert,* I (Oxford, 1955), p. 154; Theodore Gaster, *The Dead Sea Scriptures* (1957), p. 298.

9. Edward P. Blair, *Jesus in the Gospel of Matthew* (Nashville: Abingdon Press, 1960), p. 47. See also p. 85.

10. See the following treatments on this point: John Wick Bowman, *The Religion of Jesus* (Nashville: Abingdon-Cokesbury Press, 1948), esp. pp. 64 ff; U. Arthur Faus, *The Genius of Prophets* (Nashville: Abingdon-Cokesbury Press, 1946), espe. Ch. V on "The Prophets As Preachers," pp. 118-151; J. Philip Hyatt, *Prophetic Religion* (Nashville: Abingdon-Cokesbury Press, 1947), esp. Ch. XI on "Prophetic Religion," pp. 174-177.

Chapter VI

DELIVERY
Insights From the
Black Preaching Tradition

IT HAS BECOME COMMONPLACE in the church world to speak about preaching traditions as well as preaching trends. It is not unusual to even hear knowledgeable laymen refer to some minister in terms of a national or even denominational tradition in his preaching style: "Scotch," "English," "Baptist," etc. Within the last few years it has become increasingly current also to speak of a "black preaching tradition," meaning that style and manner of preaching that characterizes the preaching usually heard within the black churches in America.[1] Quite apart from the cultural interest in this area on the part of church historians, there are some significant insights to be derived from the black preaching tradition, insights which help any preacher from any tradition to sense more clearly how to keep the verbal witness of the pulpit both virile, engaging, and effective. Some of those insights are set forth in the pages to follow.

Functional

1. First, in the black church *the sermon is functional*. That is,

THE RESPONSIBLE PULPIT

the sermon is never regarded as a product for its own sake, or even as an art form, but as a means to an end. And that end? The end of the sermon as preached in the black church is to help some person: initiate someone into the faith, instruct some person on how to live, inspire some person to go on living with hope despite troubles and strain, give insight into problems and possibilities within and beyond those problems. The sermon is functional in its intent to liberate the hearer's spirit, give him life and sustain his faith.

Festive

2. Second, in the black church *the sermon is festive.* Black preaching is never abstract and tangential. It deals with concrete life, with what is experienced in the daily round, and it does so without arid speculation or poised sophistry. The black sermon is usually "playful": Playful in its measured cadences and speech liberties. The speech-result is no less true, no less sensible, even when done with "instinct" and fervid imagination. The black sermon is a kind of "soul-piece," a way of "deep calling unto deep," to use a biblical figure.

Black preaching excels in being an invitation to joy, even in the midst of sorrow and struggle. It does so by means of strong affirmation about God and good and through the contagious note of witnessed faith. Whatever festivity and playfulness fill the black sermon are there because they have been *won* in the midst of sorrow and lament, making the sermon itself an open expression of faith that has worked its way through, and now speaks in praise of God. This amounts, really, to a depth theology of soul-worship. The festivity which results in this way is never an opiate, therefore, and the playfulness is not calculated escapism. The black sermon celebrates remembered victories in the midst of raw demands.

In his book *Feast of Fools* Harvey Cox has treated the festivity theme, among other things. In placing stress on the ingredients of festivity, Cox isolates three basic ingredients: (a) calculated ex-

Delivery

cess; (b) celebrative affirmation—either "because of" or "in spite of;" and (c) juxtapositional contrast between the event and the everyday experience.[2] The black preaching tradition can be understood in part in terms of this kind of analysis, but the aspect of "playfulness" should be highlighted as a part of that calculated excess. The playfulness has to do with a lack of bondage to strict objectivity, a way of exposing subjectivity in the interest of personal witness—which shares the contagion of involvement. The personal element is immediately obvious and strong. This open commendation of the truth rescues the statement from coldness and a forbidding formalism. There is no fear to talk about religious experience, even to refer to one's own experiences if this can better serve the truth. To be sure, if the black preacher cannot so call attention to his own experience—adding his own word to that of the biblical witness, he is not regarded as an authentic spokesman for God. This is why the concept of a "call" to preach continues to this day as a living factor in black worship circles. When the call is festively regarded, and when the preacher appeals to his experience as a knowing witness, a sense of authority is conveyed; the preacher speaks as one who knows "from the inside." This is important to those who hear his words, moving as they do from worship to face life. His high expressiveness and festive freedom helps to renew his hearers, remind them, "reach" them, and deepen their roots of faith.

Those who make battle daily on the many fronts of personal and public life need a worship occasion that both informs and inspires them. What worshiper can be untouched and unmoved by the preacher's recital of the victories of faith? Who does not rejoice to *sense* the truth that his present moment, however dark and forbidding, is not the last moment? Who cannot sense the joy of freedom when he realizes that the contradictions of life are not final contradictions, that the possibilities which remain are many and not yet exhausted by any means? Who can fail to anticipate victories when the assurance registers that goodness and mercy will follow him? All of this keeps the biblical tradition of "good

THE RESPONSIBLE PULPIT

news" alive in the gathered church. The play element is important in it all, but it is the play of sentiment, suggestion, and a serious faith that rejoices in God.

Communal

3. A third characteristic in the black preaching tradition is its *communalism*. The sermon must aid the sense of group life. The well-known tradition of call-and-response should be understood in this light.[3] Many churches of varying denominational contexts are accustomed to plan a call-response action through a reading, a litany, a chant; the black sermon is itself a call for response. The black preacher usually allows for and expects acts of communalism among his hearers, even vocal expressions of praise, agreement, encouragement, and prompting. The speaker's word alerts, calls, promises, energizes, bestows, blesses, challenges, corrects, confutes, chastises, claims, convicts, convinces. Although specific responses among black church audiences will vary in keeping with many factors (educational levels, size of church, denominational orientation, social setting, age groupings, to name only a few), it is not infrequent that audible expressions of response will occur in most black settings where the preacher speaks with festive bearing, for a functional purpose, and with a sense of community with his hearers.

Communalism is also evident in the musical portion of the worship service. There is something more here than just group singing or everyone singing the same song or hymn in the harmony of sound and rhythm. There is actual and contagious engagement with each other in the music. James H. Cone has commented on this, saying that "Black music is unity music," explaining, "Black music is unifying because it confronts the individual with the truth of black existence and affirms that black being is possible only in a communal context."[4] The black sermon is itself somewhat musical at times, with a basic rhythm to its cadences and tonal variations that energize, envelope, and stir the worshipers to share their faith

Delivery

even emotionally. This aspect of the black tradition is akin in some ways to the Hebrew concept of the creative power of the spoken word. This proclivity to the oral is part of an evident concern for community, with words being used to generate both vision and sense, fundamental understanding and emotional direction.

Radical

4. Fourth, the nature of preaching in the black church calls for the sermon to be *radical*: it must take the hearer to the roots of personal life and vital response. More often than not, this radicality demands that the preacher be a man of courage.

There is a story that has been preserved about the radicality of Dr. William Holmes Borders of Atlanta, Georgia. The story tells about a message Borders gave during the 1948 Georgia Baptist Convention, held at Pelham, a small but problematic town in that state.[5] As principal speaker, Borders used the occasion for a major thrust against the ungodly system of segregation, urging more militancy against it, and telling his black hearers that it was time for them to stand up to whites. The whole town soon heard about Borders' statements and a white mob gathered outside the church where the convention was being held. Borders preached on, seemingly oblivious to possible danger to himself and the group. Speaking on, he advised not only courage but politeness, wedding the radical offensiveness of his stand for rights with the reasonableness of peaceful means.

There are other stories about his radicality in the pulpit. Preaching on "True Religion," Borders has often used the most effective illustrations to make his points clear on what constitutes true religion. For his introduction Borders isolated several types of religion: tribal religion, state religion, Sunday religion, and real religion. On the matter of tribal religion he warned against practicing a brotherhood that excluded those of another race or color. He illustrated the point by the story of a black man who was hungry, forced to beg for food because he had been denied all opportunites which would have prepared him for an independent life. He rang

THE RESPONSIBLE PULPIT

the front doorbell of a southern mansion and the owner of the house answered. "I'm hungry," the black man pleaded. The white man answered, "Go around to the back door." Some food was prepared inside and finally brought to the black man standing at the back door. The white man said, "First we will bless the food. Now you repeat after me, 'Our Father . . .'" The black man began, "Your Father . . ." The white man corrected him, *"Our* Father . . ." The black man repeated his own words, "Your Father . . ." The white man asked him why he refused to be corrected. The black beggar replied, "Well, boss, if I say 'Our Father,' that would make you and me brothers, and I'm 'fraid the Lord wouldn't like it, you makin' your brother come to the back porch to get a piece of bread."[6] The point was clear. He had spoken a radical truth but with the logic of humor. What he preached had the character of radical proclamation and he risked all to speak it.

As for "radicality" on the part of the preacher, these words of Rudolf Bultmann explain and highlight that characteristic:

> Proclamation is *personal address*. It is authoritative address, the address of the word of God, which, paradoxically, is spoken by a man, the preacher. As God's representative (cf. 2 Cor. 5:20), the preacher stands over against the congregation. He does not speak as its voice nor does he bring to consciousness or to clear expression whatever may slumber in his hearers in the way of ideals and feeling, yearnings or even unexpressed certainties. To be sure, he can do all this, but only in order to confront his hearers with the word of God, to place them under the shifting and judging power of the word and therewith under the promise of grace.[7]

Dr. Raymond S. Jackson has preached with strong personal concern across his ministry about the question of birth control. Even today, when the problem of "population explosion" is being discussed across the world, Jackson still holds his original frame of thought on the matter. He continues to speak personally about it because his reasons are personal. Says he, "Some of my minister

Delivery

friends who advocate birth control asked me if I believed in it. My answer was a positive No! I added, 'And if you want my personal reason, here it is: I happen to be the fourteenth child in a family of fifteen children. Consequently, if my mother had started controlling, I wouldn't be here to tell the story.' If I, the fourteenth child, had a right to life, liberty, and the pursuit of happiness, so does every other child, however large the family may be." Jackson adds, "Incidentally, I am the only minister out of that family of fifteen children!" His reasons, then, are both personal and religious.[8]

The radicality of the late Dr. Vernon Johns is well-known in black church circles. Among the many episodes used to illustrate this power on his part, there is the one Martin Luther King, Jr., Johns' successor as pastor of the Montgomery church, told me about how Johns could pour it on in telling it "like it is." The story itself dates, however, from a much earlier period in Johns' life. The pastor was asked to handle a certain funeral; the man who was being funeralized died in a brawl. The place was filled to capacity. Johns wasted no words and hence no time. He stood tall and spoke firmly—perhaps abrasively? "Any man who stops by a saloon with his paycheck instead of going home to his wife and children with it ought to be struck over the head with a baseball bat and killed. That's what happened in this man's case. You know the story. The benediction will be given at the graveside."[9] He then raised his hand in beckoning gesture toward the mortician, calling "Undertaker!" Radicality! Irritating, yes, excoriating, yes, unsettling, yes, but salvific in intent and thrust.

Radicality in the sermon engages the hearer. It makes him know that he is being confronted, that necessity is being laid upon him to respond. True preaching is always confrontational. As proclamation it is not exactly or completely dialogical. This is not to say that there is compulsion in the kerygma against which man would rightfully rebel; nor is it to say that the preacher exercises his will to power in making an arbitrary demand by his words. It is rather to say that the speaking of God's word to man is a radical act; it places man before God as a "thou" but not as an equal, as one

107

THE RESPONSIBLE PULPIT

who needs to be guided, confronted, helped, taught, disciplined, forgiven, renewed. Preaching is a special process with a special goal and end in view. Radical means are essential to that process and end.

Climactic

5. A fifth essential characteristic of black preaching is *to produce a climax of impression for the hearer.* The sermon is a functional instrument, based upon a distinctive scriptural word, calculated in faith to win and nurture the life of the hearer. A kind of feeling-attitude is important for a proper response. Zestful speech encourages this result. The will for community, and means for nurturing it, is also essential. So are mind-engaging lines. Imagination also renders its service, and continues at that service even while the process of delivery continues. Soren Kierkegaard in one of the entries in his *Journals* wrote of imagination as "what providence uses in order to get men into reality, into existence, to get them far enough out, or in, or down in existence."[10] Scripture, interpretation, zestful speech, a concern for community, mind-engaging lines, controlled imagination—all these are calculated to incite the hearer to participate as well as listen, leading him to a climax of impression for faith and life.

When the preacher appears free and festive, sound in his approach and use of Scripture; when his sermon is a kind of "open confession of his faith," an "on-the-scene" report from his heart, and a product of vision; then religion appears most real to the listening one. Feeling-attitude is best generated when the sermon betrays the preacher's experience with the truth he proclaims, when something presents itself as an evidence of his partnership with God, something of the supernatural flow in the gospel. Preaching is as much contagion as it is conversing, perhaps it is really more contagion than conversing.

Dr. Howard Thurman has been credited with giving a worship service some of the atmosphere of a concert hall. This was not a

Delivery

criticism but a compliment. The one who made the statement had often heard him preach and was quite mindful that Thurman's sermons involved him in a climax of impression. That preacher does not overdramatize his messages, nor does he depend upon mass psychology. He knows how to involve his listeners and make them share with him in a contagious moment of truth. He bends his skills to this end. Is this not what happens in a concert hall? Pianist Artur Schnabel wrote about one such occasion in a letter to his wife Therese. He had played an all-Beethoven program in England. Schnabel felt that he had made his artistry approach the vision in Beethoven's music, that he had communicated that vision. He commented to his wife, "The impression I made—on a very intelligent audience—was very interesting: tense, lost within themselves, many of those present may have experienced something like a glimpse of the Unknown."[11] As a servant of truth, the preacher is concerned with no less than this also. He seeks to produce a climate for faith and a climax of impression by which that faith begins and acts to the honor of God in the human heart.

Howard Thurman recalls some of the sermons he heard in his boyhood years. The pastor of the family church was quite adept at effective preaching. Thurman reports, "Sometimes the preacher gave graphic descriptions of hell as if he had been there on a personally conducted tour."[12] That preacher had learned to use his powers of imagination in the service of biblical realities, producing intrigue, insight, and necessary caution for life. "There was not a Sunday," Thurman adds, "when the preacher did not, in some way or another, take everybody by 'Calvary'."[13] The trip was in the service of the redemptive theme. To the sharing church, and especially to little Howard, sitting in his grandmother's lap, "The drama was exhilarating." "It was so real, so real . . ."[14] A climax of impression had been reached.

In his autobiography *Along This Way,* James Weldon Johnson has recalled a similar experience in his contact with a certain preaching service one Sunday night in Kansas City. Johnson has, however, described the service as an exhibition, pointing up the

THE RESPONSIBLE PULPIT

comic and extraneous aspects of the "evangelist's" antics and the congregation's response. Nevertheless, Johnson admitted, "I was fascinated by this exhibition; moreover, something primordial in me was stirred."[15] Although the service, such as it was, did not dispose him to worship, it did gather him in an atmosphere of creative impression. The preacher's abandon, picturesque speech, freedom in handling his materials, sonorous diction, native idioms, and syncopated rhythms so touched Johnson's imagination that before the preacher finished, Johnson took a slip of paper from his pocket and "somewhat surreptitiously jotted down some ideas,"[16] which he soon shaped into "The Creation," a sermon in verse. Johnson could not commend that exhibition as a worthy service; but he could not deny the climax of impression which he had experienced.

It is true that art can be exploited and turned to the false end of exhibitionism. But the prostitution of an art must not blind us to its proper end and effects. A preacher must not ignore the soundness of the theory *and insistence* that his sermon should produce a climax of impression for his hearers. Preaching at its best involves this, and more; but if it lacks this ability, no matter whatever else it has, such a sermon will make no difference.

NOTES

1. One of the most helpful and resourceful studies on this is found in Henry H. Mitchell, *Black Preaching* ("The C. Eric Lincoln Series in Black Religion") (Philadelphia: J. B. Lippincott Company, 1970).

2. *The Feast of Fools* A Theological Essay on Festivity and Fantasy (Cambridge, Mass.: Harvard University Press, 1969), see esp. pp. 21-26. There is some treatment of this in an earlier work by Johan Huizinga, *Homo Ludens:* A Study of the Play Element in Culture (Boston: Beacon Press, 1955). Trans. by R. F. C. Hull.

3. For a study of this and other characteristics among black audiences or congregations, see Arthur L. Smith, "Some Characteristics of the Black Religious Audience," in *Speech Monographs* (Vol. XXXVII No. 3) August 1970, pp. 207-210. For examples of the black preaching art, see Marcus H.

Delivery

Boulware, *The Oratory of Negro Leaders:* 1900-1968 (Westport, Conn.: Negro Universities Press, 1969), esp. Ch. 13, pp. 181-201.

4. *The Spirituals and the Blues:* An Interpretation (New York: The Seabury Press, 1972), p. 5.

5. Cited by S. P. Fullinwider, *The Mind and Mood of Black America:* 20th Century Thought (Homewood, Ill.: The Dorsey Press, 1969), p. 232, and based upon a witness report in *National Baptist Voice* of December 1, 1948, p. 3.

6. See James W. English, *Handyman of the Lord: The Life and Ministry of the Rev. William Holmes Borders* (New York: Meredith Press, 1967), pp. 33-34.

7. "General Truths and Christian Proclamation," in *Journal for Theology and the Church,* Vol. 4 of *History and Hermeneutic,* ed. by Robert W. Funk and Gerhard Ebeling (New York: Harper and Row, Inc., 1967), p. 153. Trans. by Schubert M. Ogden. The italics are by Bultmann.

8. See James Earl Massey, *Raymond S. Jackson: A Portrait* (Anderson, Indiana, Warner Press, 1967), p. 18.

9. Another version, slightly different, has recently been published in Charles Emerson Boddie's *God's "Bad Boys"* (Valley Forge: Judson Press, 1972), see p. 72.

10. *The Journals of Soren Kierkegaard,* ed. and trans. by Alexander Dru (London: Oxford University Press, 1938), p. 519. (Entry 1338).

11. Cesar Saerchinger, *Artur Schnabel:* A Biography (New York: Dodd, Mead and Company, 1957), p. 181.

12. Elizabeth Yates, *Howard Thurman:* Portrait of a Practical Dreamer (New York: The John Day Company, 1964), p. 35.

13. *Ibid.,* pp. 35-36.

14. *Ibid.,* p. 37.

15. *Along This Way:* The Autobiography of James Weldon Johnson (New York: The Viking Press, 1933), p. 336.

16. *Ibid.,* p. 336.

Epilogue

"Striving For the Mastery"

WHO ARE the master preachers? Opinions will vary about this, depending somewhat on the opining person's ability to assess preaching, his tastes, his conditioning, his contacts, and assessments from others whose judgments he values. Most of us have had recommendations from others whom we trusted to tell us who we should hear preach. Most of us have followed those recommendations and have found that we learned much, both from the preaching we heard and about those who gave us the advice we received; sometimes we have valued the persons who advised us much more highly than before. Basil Davenport, writer and critic, tells of reading a certain volume of poems by Stephen Vincent Benet. Benet's literary techniques fascinated the younger man who was still a schoolboy at the time. Young Davenport had gone to Benet's writings on the basis of someone's published review. As an adult and able writer he later commented about the review he had read, saying that "that was the first book I ever bought on the strength of a review—and I wish my own reviews were always as reliable as that one proved to be."[1] Many of us go to hear—or read—the sermons of others through a "review." I have heard many noble spokesmen because I was so advised by friends or fellows intent to see me blessed and my preaching benefited.

THE RESPONSIBLE PULPIT

Who are the master preachers? They are the responsible servants who so give themselves that they can preach again and again without running out of fresh and meaningful material. They are the responsible thinkers who so plan as to say the same thing a thousand times and more without banal repetition; they stay fresh, and their work is not a stale "leftover." The master preachers are those who have successfully experimented with the principles of the art of preaching, trusting those principles to help them meet men where they live and deal with them, using Scripture-wisdom, to inform and inspire them. The master preachers are those who can be specific, use particular language, and logically deal with men's daily history in the light of God's grace and saving purpose. They are those who know how to angle their approach to the persons at hand, preachers who can enter into the turmoil of the individual and speak hopefully with both a pastoral and prophetic passion. They are preachers who may or may not have published, but something kindles in the heart when they are heard. A master preacher need not be a writer, but generally when a man has mastered his art someone usually snatches one of his sermons to have it printed for a wider audience. The master preachers are those, then, who say what needs to be heard beyond the limits of the group they address.

The master preachers are those who speak to the heart with the sermon saturated by the spirit of their own worship as they speak. The master preachers are those who are most apt to be quoted by other preachers, and their sermons are pirated and plagiarized. They are men who are proud of their calling, sparing no pain to always be at their best. They are men of depth, conviction, breadth, faith, variety, challenge, commitment, and enthusiasm. They are men of reading that is both wide and rich. They are men of big themes and well-stored minds.

The great preachers are men of compassion and courage. They are men who recognize their work as a divine task, men who make the service of worship a time of dignified waiting in the presence of God. They are men more concerned about service than name or position. The great preachers, the masters of the craft, are those who lay stress upon the dignity of preaching and show that dignity through the drama of their own work in the pulpit. The master preachers are those who honor the preaching tradition from the centuries behind them and cast the vote of their own lives to shape a tradition that will follow them. The master preachers are those who, though not setting out in egotism to become acclaimed a master, nevertheless in humility and honest toil achieve that end.

NOTES

1. See *Selected Works of Stephen Vincent Benet* (New York: Farrar and Rinehart, Inc., 1942), Vol. One, Poetry, p. ix.

SERMON NOTES

SERMON NOTES

SERMON NOTES

SERMON NOTES

SERMON NOTES

SERMON NOTES

SERMON NOTES

SERMON NOTES

SERMON NOTES

SERMON NOTES

SERMON NOTES

SERMON NOTES

SERMON NOTES